MW00640122

FIND YOUR FIERCE

*Interrupt Imposter Syndrome
and Own Your Success*

TERESA SANDE

ISBN 13: 978-1-63489-410-4

Library of Congress Catalog Number has been applied for.
Printed in the United States of America
First Printing: 2021

25 24 23 22 21   5   4   3   2   1

Cover design by Zoe Norvell
Interior design by Patrick Maloney

Wise Ink Creative Publishing
807 Broadway St NE
Suite 46
Minneapolis, MN, 55413

wiseink.com

To order, visit www.itascabooks.com or call 1-800-901-3480.
Reseller discounts available.

CONTENTS

For Erik...

My best friend,
the love of my life,
and my rock.

Thank you for making me feel
like a superstar every single day!

PREFACE

This book was written over a multiyear span and includes learnings from a variety of industries and people. In the last year or two while I've completed this book, there has been a notable shift in messages toward and about women. The messages of self-acceptance, confidence, and "Nasty Women" uniting have been prevalent. I am here for this, 110 percent. Yet it's important to preface this book and its contents by saying that imposter syndrome is not singularly about self-confidence or a lack thereof. In fact, almost everyone I've coached over the years who struggles with imposter syndrome is confident. It's very difficult to achieve high levels of success without some level of self-confidence. However, imposter syndrome is very real for very confident people. Let's face it, we can't all be the incredibly *fierce* United States Representative Alexandria Ocasio-Cortez. While I've not spoken to her (yet!), perhaps she too has experienced imposter syndrome at some point in her life.

What I do know is that it is time to dissect and understand the distinction between confidence and the occasional feelings that you're a fraud and it's only a matter of time before someone finds out and rips the achievement, the accolades, or the job out of your grasp. It's critical we understand the systems we operate within so we can learn why imposter syndrome sneaks up on even the most confident of us all. Throughout this book, you will hear story after story of where imposter syndrome snuck up on some of the most influential and successful people. Why? Systems are preprogrammed to support the majority shareholder, and in corporate America's senior-most ranks, that is still white men. This book is not about making white men wrong or bad. Not at all. It is simply to understand that most of these systems were designed by white men and therefore without some overt, conscious changing, they will continue to work for white men, while inadvertently making those who are not white men most susceptible to imposter syndrome.

To be honest, the "Self-Help" book category sort of makes me cringe. While self-care is important and I am a believer in continuing to better oneself, the term self-help can drum up images of broken people. Or at the very least, people who need help mending because they can't do it on their own. If this book provides self-help for some of my readers, I'm truly happy and there is no judgment. We all need a bit of help throughout our lives and careers. Instead, I put this book in the category of Awareness-Building. Once you know something, you can't unknow it. And once you have information you can choose whether to focus on yourself and the areas you can improve, or channel your energies toward the organizations and systems you are a part of. Perhaps you choose to do a bit of both. Systems are heavy and they certainly don't change overnight. But talented, informed, motivated, and empowered people can change them. This book is for those people, whether male or female, Black or white, senior leaders or early career rock stars.

The image on the front of this book was chosen for a reason. Zebras are powerful, beautiful, smart animals in their own right. Lions are also powerful, beautiful, smart animals. The lion is a relatively universal symbol of fierceness. It's not about changing to be more like a lion or saying anything is wrong with being a zebra. While the zebra is standing in its own strong stance, the shadow of the lion is a reminder of the fierceness that is within each of us and what others often see when they look at us. You are fierce. This book is here to support you in discovering (or rediscovering) that and navigating whatever systems you are a part of to fight the fraud feelings of imposter syndrome and *find your fierce*!

INTRODUCTION

SOMETIMES I FEEL LIKE A FRAUD

My first brush with imposter syndrome came when I landed my first big job out of grad school. Getting a job offer with Intel and realizing I was about to start my career in a huge, recognizable, important company triggered my fraud feelings in a way that was so acute, I couldn't ignore it. If I'm being honest, when I think back on my life, imposter syndrome showed up many times before the Intel job offer moment, but it wasn't until I kicked off my career that it knocked me down so hard, I almost couldn't get back up, and I had no choice but to figure out what the heck was happening. Let me tell you a brief story about the course of my life and the situations that led me to that fateful imposter syndrome episode when I was about to report to work at Intel.

My dad was a police officer for thirty-plus years, and my mom was a stay-at-home mom who helped with her parents' business (running a tavern). After graduation, my brother became a teacher. All were successful in their own ways. Growing up in Milwaukee as a kid, I remember passing by tall office buildings downtown and wondering, *What happens in those buildings?* Hundreds, maybe thousands, of people walked in and out of those buildings every day, and they all had jobs in business, whatever that meant. I had never been exposed to a corporation or a large business setting like that. It wasn't something I had any knowledge of.

After graduating with my master's degree in organizational effectiveness and communication, I started searching for my first big job. I applied for a job at Intel. I'm talking about *the* Intel. At the time, this was the great big company that made computer chips and had literally hundreds of thousands of employees worldwide. The company that made everyone's computer work. The company that gave every other company their technology. The company with the Blue Man Group, for heaven's sake! It was so cool, and I had absolutely no idea what I was doing. But I landed a job, and I was so excited. I almost couldn't believe that I would become one of those people who walked in and out of a big, fancy office building every day. I was going to be a businesswoman!

The night before my first day of work, I sat on the living room floor of my tiny one-bedroom apartment, sorting through some requisite paperwork. As I completed the mundane tasks to prepare for the next day, I felt excited and proud of myself for landing my first big job. But soon my mind began to convince me I didn't belong in the job they offered me. I heard the voice in my head asking what seemed like reasonably good questions: *What do you really know about corporate America, anyway? You don't even know what happens in those big buildings every day. What do you think you're doing, and who exactly do you think you are? People are going to realize right away they've made a mistake.* My brain started to ruminate on the worst possible scenarios.

I envisioned myself walking through the doors and meeting my new team. I would say hello, tell them my background, and explain what my new role was. As I thought about the next day, I started to feel warm. No, hot. I envisioned smirks from the new people I met. I saw squinting eyes as they scrutinized my qualifications. I imagined the knowing glances they would exchange with one another when they successfully played a round of stump-the-chump at my expense. It was surely going to be a disaster.

I didn't get much sleep that night because I felt like a fraud. I believed I'd somehow tricked them all into thinking I could do the job they hired me to do, and that I would be found out within a week of starting, maybe less. Of course, that didn't happen. But this experience and others I've had throughout my career helped me as I coached people— from early career up-and-comers to C-suite executives.

WE ARE NOT ALONE

Don't worry, you aren't going crazy and you aren't alone. If you've ever experienced anything similar, there is a name for it: imposter syndrome. According to a review article published in the *International Journal of Behavioral Science*, it's estimated that at least 70 percent of the United States population has experienced what researchers call the imposter phenomenon or imposter syndrome. It's a feeling that you are a fraud and that it's only a matter of time before someone figures out you aren't as good as they thought you were.

This experience of feeling like you'll be exposed for being a fraud doesn't discriminate. It affects everyone from students to professionals, all genders, and people from a diverse array of cultural and socioeconomic backgrounds. Women tend to suffer from it in ways that have greater impact on their careers because most work cultures are not set up to support those experiencing self-doubt. In fact, many of these environments feed and intensify it, particularly for women.

Across a wide variety of industries, I found imposter syndrome was a common thread that limited these powerful women. After my own significant experiences with imposter syndrome and seeing it impact so many people who clearly had the potential to change the world, I knew I had to do something. I set out on a mission to understand what causes it and help people struggling with it.

Imposter syndrome is rampant among high-performing, high-potential women, and ironically, it shows up at times of achievement, when a woman is recognized for her strengths and accomplishments. It wreaks havoc on her confidence and keeps her from speaking up, stepping out, and standing in her greatness with authority. The crazy thing is, the very organizations that want to promote women and have greater balance with gender equity and representation may inadvertently contribute to the issue because of their biases and blind spots. It's time to dig in and assess what's going on here.

Female leaders across the world have admitted to experiencing imposter syndrome, including World Health Organization Chief Dr. Margaret Chan, Facebook COO Sheryl Sandberg, and three-quarters of female Harvard Business School students. All these women report that they've felt they don't belong in the job, role, or graduate school they're in. They live with a fear that sooner or later they're going to be found out and asked to leave.

It isn't only businesswomen or people in academia who experience it either. Some of our culture's biggest stars live with imposter syndrome. In an interview on *60 Minutes*, Academy Award–winner Jodie Foster said she feared she'd have to give her Oscar back after winning best actress for *The Accused*. "I thought it was a fluke," she said in the interview. "[I felt] like an imposter, faking it, that someday they'd find out I didn't know what I was doing. I didn't. I still don't. [It was] the same way when I walked on the campus at Yale. I thought everybody would find out."

Another famous actress and activist, Emma Watson, who won our hearts as heroine Hermione Granger in the famous *Harry Potter* series, has been quoted as saying, "It's almost like the better I do, the more my feeling of inadequacy actually increases, because I'm just going, any moment, someone's going to find out I'm a total fraud, and that I don't deserve any of what I've achieved."

Michael Uslan, the producer of the *Batman* movies, shared in a *Huffington Post* interview that when he was on set, he had serious bouts of imposter syndrome. He referenced how acute the feelings were for him at times on set, saying he would "have this background feeling that one of the security guards might come and throw me out."

And the beloved author, poet, and speaker Maya Angelou once said, "I have written eleven books, but each time I think, 'uh oh, they're going to find out now. I've run a game on everybody, and they're going to find me out.'"

The list of examples goes on. I don't know about you, but it absolutely shocked me to hear these amazingly talented people, with their long lists of accomplishments, struggle with imposter syndrome. In a strange way, it made me feel a little better that I wasn't alone. (Misery loves company?) But that feeling of comfort was short lived. If they made millions of dollars and were loved the world over, what hope was there for me or any of us regular Joes and Joannes to fight the fraud? Time to understand what this crazy phenomenon is so we can dismantle it and find our fierce.

WHAT IS IMPOSTER SYNDROME?

The tendency for people to feel like frauds was originally dubbed "imposter phenomenon" by psychologists

Pauline Clance and Suzanne Imes, who published a study, "The Imposter Phenomenon in High-Achieving Women: Dynamics and Therapeutic Intervention," in the 1978 journal *Psychotherapy: Theory, Research & Practice.* Clance and Imes worked with high-achieving women in academia and started to see a trend: despite these women's scholastic honors, test scores, earned degrees, and personal and professional accomplishments, they were not able to own their success. When asked, the women attributed their successes to luck or external factors. Clance and Imes reported that women said their achievements were due to:

- Being in the right place at the right time
- Getting selected because the first choice wasn't available
- Charming the decision-makers
- Getting lucky because of an error made by selection committees

They wrote, "Despite outstanding academic and professional accomplishments, women who experience the imposter phenomenon persist in believing they are really not bright and have fooled anyone who thinks otherwise. Numerous achievements, which one might expect to provide ample object evidence of superior intellectual functioning, do not appear to affect the imposter belief."

The key word here is *belief.* You see, beliefs are immensely powerful things that come from the mindsets we develop as children and young adults. The mind can convince us of many things that aren't true but that we believe to be true. For example, if you believe you did a terrible job on a presentation, it doesn't matter how many people tell you it was incredible. If you don't believe it, you won't listen. As far as you're concerned, it was terrible.

As popular culture took hold of this concept, other writers and researchers dubbed the experience "imposter syndrome," which Clance and Imes adamantly opposed. They argued these feelings were not indications of a syndrome that should be listed in the *Diagnostic and Statistical Manual of Mental Disorders* and fixed with medication—they were indicators of a mindset that can cause certain emotions and behaviors. As this concept has become more mainstream, though, it is mostly referred to as imposter syndrome, so for the purposes of this book, I refer to it as such.

Whether you call it imposter syndrome or imposter phenomenon, this underlying belief system is alive and well, and I've watched these behaviors blow up careers when they go unchecked or unresolved. I've teetered on the edge of that cliff myself, and I don't want it to happen to you.

Since those original research studies, many other researchers have augmented Clance and Imes's work. Though there's still debate about exactly what imposter syndrome is, most researchers agree it's a form of social anxiety in which people look outside themselves for a sense of validation and approval.

WHAT DOES IMPOSTER
SYNDROME LOOK LIKE?

Back in the 1970s, Clance and Imes identified four common behaviors that showed up when women experienced the imposter phenomenon:

- **Working too hard.** Women micromanaged their teams, sought to control their environment or other people, put in way more hours than anyone else, and triple-checked work to overcompensate for their perceived lack of expertise.

- **Trying to please other people.** Women who used to be confident in their ideas began to tell people what they wanted to hear instead of sharing their brilliance.

- **Looking for external validation.** Instead of turning inward for validation, they made extreme efforts to gain approval or to be liked by others.

- **Acting a part.** Women modified their actions to fit what they perceived to be socially acceptable for their gender—not too assertive, not too outspoken, and not too masculine.

The more I learned about imposter syndrome, the more I saw these behaviors in the women I coached. I started talking with them about it. In these conversations, I would hear a big sigh of relief followed by, "Yes, that's me! You mean there's a name for it? I'm not alone and I'm not crazy! OK, so, now what?" It's important to understand how to tune out the signals that make you feel like you aren't good enough so you can focus on your strengths.

EXAMPLE, PLEASE?

Allow me to walk you through the experience of someone in the throes of imposter syndrome. The next story is based on many of the successful women I've coached and worked with over the years. It illustrates how imposter syndrome shows up, how subtle it can be, and the behavior-changing impact it has on people.

You finally earn that promotion you've worked so hard for, and the congratulation messages flood in as soon as the announcement is sent to your colleagues. Mary sends a nice email saying, "There's no one better to do this job." Paul stops you in the hall and says, "Thank goodness you're going to be in this role. Now we'll finally have the strong leadership we need." Karla sends an instant message saying, "Hey lady! It's about time, you totally deserve this." It feels good . . . pass the champagne!

A day or two goes by, and you're about to move into your new office. The excitement of the initial accomplishment starts to wear off and some negative self-talk creeps in. Emails come in requesting a few key decisions from you. An approval is needed to move a big project forward and you're now the approver. You don't have all the necessary background to make the decision yet. How could you? You've only been in the job a few days!

Your new peer, Christopher, stops by, and during the conversation you sense he isn't happy you're in this role. It took him eight years to be promoted to this level, but you were promoted after only two. The conversation ends with Christopher letting you know this job isn't going to be a "walk in the park." You think, *Thanks for the warm welcome.*

After a particularly exhausting first week, you stare at your computer screen and start doubting yourself. You worry senior management made the wrong selection. Sure, you're talented and have a lot of strengths, but what if you haven't learned everything you need to be successful in this job? You also know your successes have come by having a fantastic team, and it always seems to be a strong group effort that gets those results, not just you by yourself. If that's true and they've made the wrong choice, what will happen when they figure out you aren't the rock star everyone thinks you are? What if you mess up?

A month goes by, and while things are going well overall, there was an omission in the first budget draft you submitted. One of your employees missed a line item and you didn't see the error. Christopher points it out for you, the entire team, and your new boss in a leadership team meeting. In a phone call with one of the higher-ups, you're asked for your opinion about what to do with the operations in Brazil. You share your ideas, but don't know all the details yet, so you only stammer out a few things.

You're sure you sounded like an idiot. That evening, you play over in your mind what you wished you would have said, and you don't get a lot of sleep.

A week later, you have a vacation planned with your family. Nothing fancy, but it's a chance to get away and disconnect for a while. You don't feel things are where they need to be at work, so you tell your spouse it would be better to postpone the trip. It's nearing the end of the calendar year, and the vacation policy is "use it or lose it." While you know you won't get your time off counted before the end of the year, you simply can't let go of control in the office. The stakes are too high. You don't take that vacation, lose the paid time off, and everyone is relatively unhappy with the decision—including you.

The following Monday, Richard, one of your employees, comes to you with his resignation letter. While it's nothing personal, he wanted the job you got, and he's been waiting nearly five years for that promotion. He's taking his talents elsewhere. At this point, you're feeling pretty sure the company has made a big mistake in putting you in this role, and it's only a matter of time before people find out you're not as good as everyone thought you were.

You've always trusted your team members in the past to make good decisions, but now you feel you can't risk looking like you don't know what's happening in your business unit, so you dive in and start managing the day-to-day details. You comb over every line of the budget when it comes in and question the minutiae. By doing this, you're convinced people will see that you know your stuff and you're leading this work. You're no fraud. This takes a lot of your time and energy. Meanwhile, your team is growing frustrated.

In another staff meeting, when Christopher points out a slight 1 percent dip in performance for the business unit you now lead—essentially the equivalent of a rounding error—you snap back and are defensive in your response and justification. This is uncharacteristic of you.

When a team member mentions how sad they are that Richard left the company, you nod but secretly feel guilty and responsible for his departure. After all, it's because you were promoted into the job he wanted that he decided to leave. And now here you are not exactly knocking it out of the park. You think to yourself that this may be further reinforcement that you don't belong in this role.

When you get home, you realize you've forgotten that your child needs supplies for a school event in the morning that you were supposed to attend. But now, you decide you can't go because you don't want your new team thinking you're not committed to your work. Your daughter says it's OK, but you know she's disappointed, and it eats away at you. Another night of low-quality sleep.

The next time you're invited to a senior executive meeting, you stay up until the wee hours of the morning trying to memorize every possible detail that might come up. When you arrive at the meeting, the executives simply want to talk about a strategic philosophical alignment between the current culture and the company they're considering acquiring. While in the past you would have jumped all over this discussion, because you love people, culture, strategy, and organizational dynamics, instead you sit quietly and don't add much to the conversation. You hold back and wait to be asked for your input. When asked directly for your opinion, you try to work in some of the details you memorized the night before and are met with a few blank stares. They weren't looking for the facts and details, they wanted your insights and ideas. Your brilliance.

This isn't who you are. This isn't how you operate. These aren't the behaviors that made you stand out as a top talent and made leadership want to promote you. You wonder, *Why am I feeling and acting this way? What. Is. Happening?*

WHAT IS HAPPENING?

What's happening is imposter syndrome. When a smart, powerful, and courageous woman grows in leadership, she often finds herself in a stretch role. And to learn, she has to return to a state of curiosity in which she doesn't have all the answers. This kind of state is not new to her, but because she's higher up the ladder, the stakes are higher. Not having all the answers feels less acceptable to her now. She feels like a fraud. She worries someone will find out she isn't as great as they thought she was.

Sound familiar? Do you ever feel the "fraud" creep in? Don't panic. I can help you fight the fraud.

Dr. Valerie Young is one of the foremost experts on imposter syndrome, having written extensively on the topic. In her book *The Secret Thoughts of Successful Women*, Dr. Young categorizes people fighting imposter syndrome into five primary groups, which you will see illustrated throughout the stories in this book:

- **The Perfectionist**: Someone who strives to be their best, no matter the cost; they set unrealistic standards for themselves.

- **The Superwoman/Superman**: Someone with an almost addiction-like struggle with their work; they compare themselves to their coworkers, pushing themselves as hard as possible.

- **The Natural Genius**: Someone who sets out to achieve perfect results, with a very lofty goal, on their first try; they feel frustrated, shameful, or unworthy if the task doesn't come easily to them.

- **The Soloist**: Someone who can't ask others for help; they feel they aren't competent if they need help and that they need to prove their worth through extreme productivity.

- **The Expert**: Someone who feels like they never

measure up. They need to know all the answers or information on a topic; otherwise, they feel they pale in comparison to their peers.

WHY THIS BOOK AND WHY NOW?

As I held workshops and coached women to help them own their success, I could not have guessed the nerve it would strike. I was shocked by the large numbers of people who approached me after workshops to tell me stories about how they felt like a fraud too. They shared how imposter syndrome impacted their lives and careers. Each interaction left me feeling frustrated. I wanted to help. And though many people have written about imposter syndrome and the fact that it exists, I found very little actionable material to help people fight it. It's my sincere hope that this book gives you reasonable steps you can take to fight the fraud, own your success, and find your fierce!

In addition to the women I was working with and coaching, at the core, my career has had an underlying focus on organizational effectiveness. I've spent years working with leaders to make sure their organizations ran as effectively as possible to enable strong performance and achieve their goals. I've seen time and again a sense of frustration from these organizations. A frustration that there isn't more diversity, especially in senior-level roles. Since the early nineties, most companies have had some sort of focus on diversity and inclusion and ensuring equity across their leadership ranks. I have been fortunate to work for progressive companies who cared about this equity and took steps to drive a more inclusive environment for everyone. But I couldn't help but notice the frustration of the leaders of these organizations at times. They invested in diversity recruiting efforts, held inclusion trainings, talked about having an equal and balanced workforce that represents the customers they serve . . . yet the outcome was almost always the same: very few women, especially women of color, and people who are different from the majority of senior leaders (i.e., white men) filling top leadership positions in the organization.

We are all "girl power!" and you shouldn't have to ever apologize for who you are. I believe that, I truly do. Yet, when we settle into the corporate structures we are a part of, the playing field isn't always level—in fact, it rarely is. We want to succeed and know damn well we can. But sometimes we put on the mask to fit in. I don't want to do that any longer. You don't want to either, or you likely wouldn't be reading this book.

I no longer felt I could influence the kind of change that needs to happen by talking to one person at a time. So, I set out to write this book and reach as many people and organizations as I could. This book holds up a mirror for them, to start conversations, explore solutions, and take action. Let's stop banging our heads against the wall and wishing for a different outcome. Let's *make* a different outcome. Let's make sure imposter syndrome doesn't stop our highest-achieving, most brilliantly talented people from doing the amazing work in the world we need them to do. Together, let's fight the fraud and find your fierce!

FIGHTING THE FRAUD

YOUR FRAUD FIGHTER GUIDE

I've spent my entire career, over twenty-five years, in corporate America working in human resources for several large Fortune 50+ companies. I've worked closely with executives to coach their top talent coming up in the pipeline. Working alongside talent at the height of their careers, I've coached them to be their best.

The more women I worked with, the more I noticed those climbing the corporate ladder—who were, in fact, the best and brightest stars in the organization—experienced self-limiting beliefs and a distorted view of themselves. The higher up the ladder they went, the more they secretly felt like frauds. They saw themselves as "lucky" and attributed their success to external factors. The more their self-doubt crept in, the less successful they became—and in many cases, the rungs on the ladder started to weaken or even break.

This amazed me. How could these successful women all be experiencing the same thing? And if I was being honest with myself, why did I experience it too? I paid attention and became more self-aware about what I was doing in those times when I felt like a fraud. I realized I had a number of coping mechanisms that I used to fight it. As I coached people and mentored earlier-career talent, I shared those tips and tricks. A consistent compliment I receive is that I'm a dot connecter and systems thinker. When a problem pops up, I don't just solve the problem in front of me, I try to think of its root cause and how a solution might prevent it from ever happening again. I also think about the upstream and downstream impact of actions.

As I conducted research for this book, I found myself wondering what I was going to say that was different from the oodles and oodles of research that is already out there on so many of the topics I cover. It's true what they say: there is almost nothing new under the sun. Remembering that one of my gifts and talents is connecting dots, I took bodies of research on neural paths, happiness, self-esteem, corporate culture, gender differences, diversity, inclusion, mindsets, business results, and imposter syndrome, and I connected the dots across the research. I brought in patterns that tie together to tell a bigger story, one that I hope you will find intriguing and compelling enough to examine your own relationship with these issues.

As I delivered workshops and worked with people on these connections, and imposter syndrome in particular, they encouraged me to share my ideas more broadly. I realized that I had a number of ways I had helped myself and things that were resonating with others along the journey to fighting imposter syndrome. I'm here to share those with you. Let's talk about how this book will help you.

BUT FIRST, SOME CONTEXT . . .

Writing a book is hard, y'all. It's taken nearly ten years to do this. Kind of crazy. Why? Well, because it is hard. I have tremendous respect for naturally gifted writers and people who can take an idea or concept and breathe life into it. It's truly a gift. While I've always been told I'm a good writer, being a book writer and author is very different from being a good writer. I had a lot of ideas jumbled up in my head, but it takes a special talent to get them out on paper.

The anxiety I felt about not getting this book out for nearly ten years was fed at times by imposter syndrome. "Who am I to write a book?" was a question I asked myself and the universe more times than I care to admit. And, more than the annoyance of asking it over and over again, that question literally stopped me dead in my tracks from writing the book, more than once. Imposter syndrome stops us from doing the things we are good at, the things we are called to do, and from sharing our talents with others who could benefit from them. We must stop that!

I had something to say and lots and lots of experience and examples to draw from. I also knew I wasn't alone. I wasn't the only person feeling this way. So many people had told me about the nerve this topic struck for them. As I started to write, I knew I needed to talk to other people and include their stories and voices. I interviewed many, many people in the production of this book.

Sometimes they were formal, recorded interviews with specific questions. Other times they were heart-to-heart conversations with friends where I asked if I could share part of their story that perfectly illustrated how imposter syndrome sneaks up. Also, throughout the book are composites of the thousands of people I've worked with and coached over the years, including themes that showed up for them and plans we put in place to combat imposter syndrome. I talked with executives, teachers, mothers, men, women, people of color, students, LGBTQIA+ people, entrepreneurs, friends, and family members from all walks of life spanning multiple generations. Their stories and themes shaped this book. Their wisdom informed the solutions. My fierce comes from their fierce, and that is something we will talk about later in the book—who's in your corner when imposter syndrome rings your doorbell and tries to knock you down? By the end of this book, you'll have that support network teed up and ready to go for yourself.

Lastly, much of the research and examples are geared toward the male/female gender divide and how imposter syndrome shows up for women. It's not because others don't experience it, and it's not because the solutions won't work for anyone else. It's simply the area I have the most experience with, so I tend to focus on it throughout the book. But the overarching intent of this book is to be inclusive and invite people into this conversation.

Imposter syndrome impacts people from all different backgrounds, and I want everyone to find their fierce!

THE FIND YOUR FIERCE FRAIMWORK

I developed a system to help you navigate what is happening when you experience imposter syndrome. We will walk through everything you need to know to find your fierce. You will understand on a deeper level what imposter syndrome is, what causes it, how to notice it when it pops up, and ways to combat it. I will also guide you in using the Find Your Fierce FrAIMwork. It's a simple and powerful system that will help you manage and quiet imposter syndrome so it doesn't sabotage your career or short-circuit your happiness and contributions to the world. Here's how you will take AIM at this phenomenon so you can fully own your success:

frAIMwork™

A = Awareness **I** = Interruption **M** = Momentum

The frAIMwork gives you a clear roadmap to follow so you recognize when imposter syndrome is happening, understand its triggers, and empower yourself to shut it down.

- **Awareness:** The first step is to understand imposter syndrome and the impact it has on people and organizations. In this section of the book, you'll discover what drives these feelings and what they look like in action. You'll also learn what impact imposter syndrome has on your career, so you see the real costs associated with behaviors that come from feeling like a fraud. You'll also see what imposter syndrome costs organizations.

- **Interruption:** The second step is to learn ways to interrupt imposter syndrome when it's happening to you. In this section of the book, you will learn how to use evidence-based tools that tap into the neuroplasticity of the brain and see how you can quickly change course in the moment and choose more empowered actions. These are short-term, quick tactics for success in the moment you need them most.

- **Momentum:** The third step is to create long-term strategies to transform your relationship with imposter syndrome so it doesn't affect your ability to step up and stand out. This is the deep work. You must really know who you are and your worth to knock imposter syndrome out for good.

HOW TO USE THIS BOOK AND
HOW IT WILL HELP YOU

Geared toward anyone who has suffered from imposter syndrome, seen it in others, and is looking to find their fierce, this book is organized into three core parts following the frAIMwork. Within each part are pieces of research, stories from interviews conducted for the book, and Find Your Fierce exercises to challenge you to reflect, think differently, and take action. It's recommended to read it in its entirety to see how all the parts fit together. That said, it can also be used as a reference guide. Once you understand the concept of the frAIMwork, when imposter syndrome jumps out at you, you can give it the one-two punch by leveraging this book as your guide when you need it most.

Individuals will find this book helpful as a self-help guide to navigating imposter feelings, as well as living within the systems that create and fuel imposter syndrome. In addition, leaders and organizations will find this book helpful and eye-opening as a means of understanding why some of your top talent may be suffering. So, it's for individuals, but since individuals make up systems and organizations, they will benefit too!

Awareness is the first step to the empowerment that will free you from feelings of self-doubt, because it gives you the opportunity to choose. Without awareness, it's easy to hang out in victim mode. Once you understand what's going on, you can do something about it.

As we progress through the book and navigate the frAIMwork, each section has a Find Your Fierce exercise to help you on your journey. You will be asked to reflect and journal. A lot. Now is a good time for your very first Find Your Fierce exercise!

Find Your Fierce Exercise: Go out and invest in a fantastic pen and beautiful journal to house your reflections and thoughts. Maybe pen and paper isn't your jam. Perhaps it's time for a new iPad? This is not a frivolous purchase; this is an investment in your fierce. This is an investment in the new self-talk you are going to start listening to. This will quiet your negative self-talk. Go ahead, I'll wait . . . I can't wait to see what you get!

Ready to find your fierce? Let's get to it.

PART ONE

AWARENESS

noun

aware·ness | \ ə-ˈwer-nəs \

Definition of _awareness_***

the quality or state of being aware; knowledge and
understanding that something is happening or exists

*from Merriam-Webster Dictionary

1

CAUSES OF IMPOSTER SYNDROME

Now that we know about imposter syndrome and what it looks like in action, we need to talk about where the heck it comes from. Most people experiencing imposter syndrome are accomplished, self-aware people who are knocking things out of the park daily, whether they feel that way or not. Yet, more times than they care to think about, they feel like a fraud, like they don't belong. Unfortunately, there isn't one cause; there's typically more than one root issue at play.

Imposter feelings can torment people who experience lower self-esteem, self-worth, or self-doubt, but that doesn't mean all people experiencing these feelings aren't confident in their abilities. This is one of the great paradoxes of imposter syndrome. A woman can be both extremely aware of and confident in her talents at the same time she's struggling to feel a sense of true belonging and value at her core.

Imposter syndrome is created and triggered by a

variety of complex factors and circumstances, including things like:

- your personal beliefs and expectations
- culture and family
- gender styles and assumptions
- corporate cultures and blind spots

The list includes big items and feels daunting. The causes are vast and at times hard to navigate. It's important to dive into a few of these in detail and understand them more fully, so we will do that in the coming chapters. First and foremost, an overarching cause of imposter syndrome is your mindset.

Stanford University psychologist Carol Dweck, PhD, is the author of *Mindset: The New Psychology of Success*. She is particularly known for her work on the psychological trait of mindset. In multiple studies, she observed that humans tend to have one of two ways they think about their abilities:

- **Fixed Mindset:** In a fixed mindset, people believe their basic qualities, like their intelligence or talent, are fixed traits. They spend their time documenting their intelligence or talent instead of developing them. They also believe that talent alone creates success—without effort. This mindset can lead to a tremendous amount of fear.

- **Growth Mindset:** Individuals who believe their talents can be developed—through hard work, good strategies, and input from others—have a growth mindset. They tend to achieve more than those with a more fixed mindset. This is because they worry less about looking smart, and they put more energy into learning. This view creates a love of learning and a resilience that is essential for great accomplishment.

Clance and Imes, the researchers who identified the imposter phenomenon, must have been aware of Dweck's work, as they saw the fixed mindset at work within their study subjects. Having a growth mindset over a fixed mindset is a key element to an individual's success. Fundamentally, it is the understanding that we can develop our abilities and intelligence. We can change, grow, and be fierce.

Let's be honest, no one—especially high-achieving, awesome people—wants to believe they have a fixed mindset, but the truth is we all have a combination of both mindsets. We might have a growth mindset in our relationship with a partner but a fixed mindset around money. Or a growth mindset about our career but a fixed mindset about travel. Dweck has described several fixed-mindset triggers: "When we face challenges, receive criticism, or fare poorly compared with others, we can easily fall into insecurity or defensiveness, a response that inhibits growth." This is called a scarcity mentality.

Once you start to achieve success, the expectations

and pressure mount. It's at this very same time you would benefit the most from a growth mindset. But a growth mindset requires the ability to learn, stumble, grow, and learn some more—a state that many women trying to prove themselves in a new, bigger role feel they can't afford—and frankly, many organizations don't overtly support. In these moments, many of us pop into the fixed mindset where fear of being found out lives. Feelings of being a fraud.

A rock-star, high-achieving, senior-positioned woman feels like an imposter because she looks around at her colleagues and doesn't see a lot of people who look like her. And if we are talking about a woman of color, she sees even fewer who represent her or worse yet, no one else like herself among her peer set. She puts on a brave face, but inside she starts second-guessing her credibility and doubting her capabilities. She doesn't want to shine a light on how she's feeling or have to ask for help. She starts to act and show up differently with her team, maybe even with her family. Eventually, she wonders if she is a rock star after all.

Remember, in the frAIMwork, Awareness is the first step and the most important if you want to put imposter syndrome in its place. Having a basic growth mindset about this topic will allow you to be open to what is really going on. Let's examine these common roots of imposter syndrome so we can better understand it and how it shows up.

2

PERSONAL BELIEFS AND EXPECTATIONS

Beliefs and expectations chart our course. Expectations often stem from beliefs. If you believe rain is typically cold and makes you shiver, on that first spring day when you walk outside and it's raining, you expect to shiver. When it's a warm spring rain, our expectation is challenged or not met. Perhaps in that example it's a pleasant surprise, but it surprises us nonetheless to feel warm while it's raining. Because of your previously held belief about rain being cold, you will take certain actions. You'll wear a sweater under your raincoat and bring a hat to keep your head both dry and warm. If you walk outside and find that it is a warm rain you may feel sweaty, sticky, or uncomfortable because you took certain actions based on your belief and expectations of what that rainy day was going to feel like. Our personal beliefs and expectations about how things should be done or how something should turn out are a big reason we get tripped up by imposter feelings. If you believe you don't belong and expect that someone is going to find you out, you will be stuck in the imposter cave.

TRIPPING OVER BELIEFS

In my coaching and mentoring sessions, I heard women describe in story after story all the ways their own personal beliefs and expectations held them back when they went unchecked.

I interviewed Emily, who was COO at a leadership development company. At the time of our interview, she had recently discovered that she held the belief that she needed to know all the answers to questions that came up, or she felt like a failure. As chief operating officer, she believed that she was expected to play that role. No one explicitly told her that, but it had been her subconscious belief.

"I don't experience imposter syndrome with the big stuff because I feel like with the big stuff, I put in the time and the research to feel like I've got it right," she explained. "Where I experience it the most is in the day-to-day, small, follow-up items. For example, when my team is looking for a vision and needs an immediate response, I fight with my own need to have an answer for them as opposed to finding the answer together."

As she built her career and experienced new roles that forced her to stretch outside her comfort zone, Emily struggled with not feeling good enough—especially when she felt like she was supposed to know things and didn't. "I felt like I was literally faking it. I was asked to lead a team that was on the frontlines of our business. They often needed immediate help, and if I didn't have the exact answers right away, I felt like a failure."

The problem with feeling like an imposter is that our feelings show up in our actions. Emily described this cascading negative effect. "When I get asked questions I don't know the answer to, the back of my head tingles," Emily reported. "When that happens in meetings, I stop listening to what's going on around me, and I really narrowly focus on proving why I should be there. I start thinking, 'What's the right question to ask here? What's the information I need to share to justify my presence?' I'm so much less effective as a leader when I'm thinking about how I can sound really smart with the next thing I'm going to say." As she told me this story, I pictured her feeling like a rabbit that was being chased down by a cheetah, needing to outsmart the hunter at every turn. The awareness of when imposter syndrome showed up for Emily, as indicated by the head tingling, was key to her being able to short-circuit it and put it in its place.

We are one big integrated system—our bodies, our minds, our emotions. If we begin thinking fearful thoughts about how we have to prove we're smart enough to be in the room, fear triggers the body to react. In a case like Emily's, our body is telling us that it believes there's danger somewhere nearby—even though it's only happening in our mind. We start to prepare to respond to the perceived threat. Our head may start tingling, and this reaction takes the part of our brain that is used to thinking rationally offline. We are no longer able to think creatively, see patterns, discern what is real versus perceived. We get tunnel vision and are narrowly focused on the perceived threat at hand. Our energy is redirected to deal with the threat.

EXPECTATION REACTIONS

In the 1920s, American physiologist Walter Cannon, a professor and department chair at Harvard Medical School, coined the term "fight or flight" to explain the two primary acute responses to a stressful situation. His theories were explained in his book *The Wisdom of the Body*, published for the first time in 1932. Since then, others have built on and further refined his work through greater observation of how people react to threats or stress. It's now widely thought that there are four common responses: fight, flight, freeze, or fawn.

- **Fight:** In the fight response, we want to fight the predator. In basic terms, we are extremely fearful, and our reaction is to fight for our lives. When this happens, you get a burst of energy that might feel like superhuman strength. You fight the threat aggressively and come out swinging.

- **Flight:** Another fear-based response is to run away from the threat. You get a burst of energy here too, and that energy can power your legs to literally run away if needed. You leave the danger in the rearview mirror and don't look back.

- **Freeze:** When this response happens the body tenses up, and much like a frightened animal, you are unable to move or take action against the threat. Although it doesn't look like much on the outside, our body's nervous system is on high function. A release valve needs to be found, or this pent-up energy and stress can show up physically and mentally for the person.

- **Fawn:** This response may be the most confusing of all of them. When fawning is the response, you comply with the threat as a way to protect and save yourself. While you don't like the threat or stress, you give in to it as a survival mechanism.

Regardless of which stress response you tend to fall into, the goal is to avoid or at least minimize the threat or danger and take back control of the situation. This requires getting your brain to a state of psychological safety and awareness. If your case is like Emily's, you need to get back to and stay in the part of your brain that's able to think in expansive and innovative ways. You can do that by interrupting the stress cycle in your body using the many tools in the upcoming Interrupt and Momentum sections of this book. It's important to note, this won't happen overnight. Fighting imposter syndrome is not a one-and-done kind of deal. You will have to interrupt yourself multiple times during the course of a meeting to retrain your brain and body that there's no cheetah running after you.

Emily expected herself to always know the answers. Talk about pressure! Other than maybe Olympians or professional athletes, most human beings don't thrive when they have to be perfect. And even those athletes aren't perfect. We idolize them as though they are, but they have doubts too. Recall those celebrities mentioned earlier in the book who felt like people were going to find out they weren't as amazing as everyone thought they were. When you feel scrutinized, it's particularly difficult to excel. It's like wearing and being weighed down by cement shoes. In this case, the one scrutinizing her work was her own inner critic. Emily had told herself it was intolerable to show she didn't know something in front of others.

This fear that she would be found out affected not only her ability to lead her team, but also her ability to work collaboratively. "I'm afraid to show in the moment that I don't know what's happening," she said. "If I were more comfortable and confident, I think I'd ask more specific questions. I would really dig into things, but instead, I'll listen in the meeting and think, 'I'll figure it out on my own.'"

She acknowledged this habit is not effective and at times held her back. "I shut down in the moment. I think I'll need to circle back and so it takes longer. If I was confident in asking questions and expressing, 'I don't know what you're talking about,' we could probably solve things in the moment."

Many people are conscious of this pattern in their behavior and could take steps to start working on their tendency to not ask questions. However, it's common for people to not realize they aren't owning their awesome because they're operating with a belief system that is running the show. This takes them down a dark and ironically inaccurate path. Time to flip on the light.

As you know, Awareness is the first part of the frAIM-work. The next time you are in a meeting and you start to notice a personal belief or expectation pop up, tune in to what your "head tingling" signal is. This will be important for you to notice each time it happens so you can do something with that newfound awareness of imposter feelings.

Find Your Fierce Exercise: What are some personal beliefs and expectations you hold? Perhaps you also have felt the need to know all the answers. Write down what it means to be successful in your profession. Once you have the list generated, take a critical look at which parts of that list are factual (e.g., to prepare taxes you must have a CPA license) and which items are more your personal belief or expectation (e.g., what makes a senior leader strong is knowing the answers to questions asked of them). Place a star next to the factual items and a question mark next to the others. Reflect on where the beliefs or expectations are coming from for your items on the list that have question marks by them. Are those beliefs and expectations helping or hurting you? You have the power to take them off the list if they are not helping you.

3

CULTURE AND FAMILY

In addition to the pressures we place on ourselves and the beliefs we hold, our upbringing and the cultures that we are a part of hold a lot of power over us. It's where we receive our first messages about what is good, what is right, what is preferred. Each family is unique, and parents set the tone for what is acceptable and unacceptable for their children. In fairness to the parents out there, while there are a lot of books about parenting dos and don'ts, the reality is that you don't know how to parent until you have kids. And parenting is basically just one big experiment that everyone hopes they get right. What parents tell their kids and the messages they send them about good and bad, failure and success, are powerful.

CULTURE INFLUENCES

A friend of mine, Jacque, shared a story about her grandmother that illustrated the influence culture and family can have on the mindset of its members, even when it contradicts societal norms. Jacque's grandmother Blanche grew up in the early 1900s. At that time, Blanche's culture and the societal norms of the day dictated that education was a luxury—especially for girls in rural areas—because there was so much work to do. Like most of the young women of her generation, Blanche never graduated from high school. After she married at nineteen years old, Blanche and her husband, Emery, lived on a farm and ran that business together until the 1980s.

Jacque's mom, Jean, described Blanche as a strict, no-nonsense woman who demanded her own children take their education seriously, despite the cultural attitudes of her day. "If I came home with an A, mother would ask, 'Why wasn't it an A-plus?'" Jean said. After Blanche's death, Jean found a high school graduation announcement card from a friend of her mother's. On the outside of the envelope, Blanche had written, "When I should have graduated."

Jean said, "I had this overwhelming feeling of total sadness and love for her. She was so quiet and withdrawn. She wasn't easy to get close to, but I could suddenly see this wish of hers and understand why she'd been so hard on me." When Jean went on to college at Drake University, she earned good grades, but she felt like she was never quite enough. "I've felt imposter syndrome, for sure," she said.

By the time Jacque came along, societal rules had changed quite a bit. Women were not only encouraged to get educated but were told they could do anything—they could have it all! However, the rules passed down through the familial and cultural generations had not changed, which resulted in a certain way of looking at the world: hard work was prized. Education was highly valued. And an A was not good enough. The messages may have been subtle at times, but they never went away.

"When an A is not enough, it can easily be translated into 'I am not enough,' which is rich soil for imposter syndrome," Jacque said. Jacque attended an Ivy League college. She got a master's degree from one of the best communications schools in the country. Yet she has still spent her life with the underlying belief that an A is not enough, and it will just be a matter of time before she's found out as a fraud.

When Jacque's daughter came home from sixth grade upset about getting an A-minus on a test, Jacque tried to do something about the perfectionism that had been passed down through the generations. Jacque asked, "Did you study hard?"

"Yes," her daughter said.

"Did you learn something from what you got wrong?"

"Yes."

"Then what's the problem?"

It remains to be seen if her daughter will decide that an A is fantastic but has nothing whatsoever to do with her value as a human being. Those messages have run deep in their culture and family, and those signals show up no matter how subtle. Breaking that chain is extraordinarily difficult to do.

Jacque's story illustrates how strongly cultural rules

can shape a family's rules. It articulates very clearly the split in what a woman might know to be true about herself and the messages she receives from the world around her. It can easily lead to the distorted views women often develop about their talents and how to offer them, and what is appropriate and expected versus what is not. Though times have changed in many ways since Jacque's grandmother lived, women are still struggling with this split in what they're capable of and the cultural messages they receive about their places in the world.

Think about something as simple as how girls are socialized to:

- play nice and share
- be quiet or pretty
- don't brag or boast
- be humble

I talk to a lot of parents these days, and that is definitely shifting. There are deliberate actions being taken to level the playing field between boys and girls at a very young age, which is a positive thing to see. As a society we still aren't to a place where we have equal messages to both genders. There is still appeal to telling girls to be pretty and boys to be tough, to tell girls to be good at sharing and to tell boys to take what is theirs. Until that playing field is truly leveled, you can see what happens when fast-forwarded twenty-five years. Women share their ideas but feel uncomfortable bragging about their accomplishments. Men take what they feel they should have and demand it. This is a big, complex part of the issues of imposter syndrome and one that many books have been dedicated to.

FAMILY INFLUENCES

From the beginning, our developing brains equate the need to belong with safety. And there are many ways our sense of safety and belonging can be disrupted. Researchers, including Clance, Imes, and multiple others, discovered that some of the people who suffer from imposter syndrome feel shame when they don't meet or exceed their parents' expectations. For example, if a young girl is labeled the "smart one" in the family, she may feel the pressure to live up to the label. When she encounters situations in which she struggles, she begins to see this as evidence of her incompetence. She begins to develop extremely unrealistic expectations for herself.

According to Clance and Imes, "people who experience imposter feelings are likely to come from families in which support of the *individual* is lacking, communications and behaviors are controlled by rules, and considerable conflict is present." What I've seen and experienced is that family structures support the role the individual is supposed to play, not the actual individual themselves.

Other women reported they were praised for absolutely everything they did. Eventually, they began to distrust their parents' perceptions of them. This led them to doubt their own abilities and intelligence, facilitating their imposter beliefs. Even when women describe their childhoods as positive, they can still develop the feelings of imposter syndrome.

Sara Blakely, self-made billionaire and founder of the powerhouse brand Spanx, openly credits much of her success to her father, who encouraged his kids to fail. "We'd sit around the dinner table and he'd ask, 'What did you guys fail at this week?' If we had nothing to tell him, he'd be disappointed," she said. "He knew that many people become paralyzed by the fear of failure. My father wanted us to try everything and feel free to push the envelope. His attitude taught me to define failure as not trying something I want to do instead of not achieving the right outcome," Blakely told *Business Insider*. She went on to say, "What it did was reframe my definition of failure. Failure for me became not trying, versus the outcome." This is just one example of how our family and culture's influence is deep rooted, extraordinarily strong, and complex.

A woman interviewed for this book, Kelly, grew up in a happy, stable family. She was the middle child of three girls, and reported that when she was growing up, both of her sisters were extremely intelligent. Kelly's older sister was on the honor roll and constantly praised for her intelligence. "My family would talk to her differently than they did to me. They assumed she would be going to college and conversations were always about what she was going to do. When I came along, I was more social and less studious. When it came time to talk about college, I heard from my family that I should consider a community college. They never said, 'You're going to go to this great school and do great things.'"

Kelly's story is an example of the roles we play in our families, and how being compared to our siblings and labeled by our parents or siblings can have a dramatic impact on our beliefs about what we can accomplish. "There was never an expectation from my family that I was going to do anything fantastic with my life. To me it felt like it was because I wasn't smart enough. I wasn't an honor student. People weren't sitting around the dinner table talking about what I was going to be when I grew up like they did with my siblings," she said.

When she was young, her strengths flew under the radar. When she was six or seven, she created her own income by going door-to-door to sell her creations. This early interest in building businesses foreshadowed the tremendous success she would go on to have later in life as the president of a retail company.

While those messages didn't necessarily derail Kelly from achieving success, they have impacted her ability to own that success. After years of success as a business analyst and president, Kelly still felt like her success wasn't real. She traced it back to those early messages she received from her family. "Imposter syndrome is embedded in my own insecurities. I start thinking, *I wish I would have gone to a Big 10 school. I wish I would have focused more on advanced degrees.* I don't have an MBA and that creates insecurity for me."

Another example of how imposter syndrome showed up for her came many years after graduating from college. Kelly applied for a new role that involved a background check. During the process, she woke in a panic in the middle of the night. "I woke my husband up and asked him, 'Did I graduate from college? Did I finish it? Really?'" she said. "My husband said, 'Of course you graduated,' but I had to validate it. I literally got up the next morning and called the school to verify that I'd graduated. I didn't walk in graduation, so I didn't have this closing ceremony around it. I just graduated and moved on, but suddenly I was second-guessing myself. 'Did I ever get a paper confirmation in the mail?'" she exclaimed.

That experience opened up the opportunity for Kelly to examine her beliefs. Because she didn't have the MBA from a Big 10 school, she believed on some level her success didn't count, because she was taught there is a right way and a wrong way to be successful. "My husband said, 'You really don't recognize that you've earned the right to be where you are.' He was right. I knew that my insecurities were overtaking me, and they would prohibit me from being successful if I didn't recognize them and talk about them out loud. So I started talking with my husband and asking myself the question, 'Why would I wake up in the middle of the night feeling like a fake?'"

LESSONS LEARNED

There are two important lessons to take from Kelly's story. First, as children we craft our identities as our brains are still developing. And second, our families have a powerful and lasting effect on us. If those lessons stay in your subconscious, they undermine your successes and keep you from owning the truth that you are a rock star.

The first lesson is that we craft our identities as children when our brains are still developing, and those stories we tell ourselves about who we are and what we're capable of have a tremendous hold on us, even when our lived experiences tell us something different. Our families have lasting effects on us that can be difficult to bring to our awareness. Kelly's underlying beliefs were suddenly brought into the light of day during this experience. This new consciousness enabled her to begin a self-reflective process, which is one of the first steps toward self-mastery.

The second lesson is that our families play a major role in how we develop and internalize our ideas about who we are and what we're capable of accomplishing. When we're born, our parents, caregivers, and siblings begin to tell us stories about who we are, what our role is in the family, what the rules are, and what is expected of us. We learn quickly what will help us fit within the family structure so we won't be cast out. At the root of human development are these central concerns: How can I survive? How can I get these people to feed me / love me / care for me / pay attention to me? We don't want to be cast from the nest, so we figure out how to stay in good graces with our caregivers. We seek praise and recognition that we are doing things right and are loved.

In the early research Clance and Imes did, they discovered that family relationships play a major role in how individuals develop and internalize their self-concept. They discovered the women they studied came from two different family types, both of which affected their development of imposter feelings. One group came from a family that freely used family labels, lumping them into certain roles in the family like "the smart one," "the intelligent one," "the sensitive one," and so on.

Women from those families felt they could never prove their worth or success, regardless of their actual accomplishments.

The other group of women studied came from an environment that included what they called "undeserved praise" from their parents, where they were essentially praised for everything they did. Eventually, that group began to distrust their parents' perceptions as inaccurate or false. This eventually led to the women in that group doubting their abilities and intelligence, further reinforcing the belief that they were imposters or not as good as their families said they were.

SOCIAL FOUNDATIONS

The millennial stereotype says this generation has a tremendous need for recognition. This stems from being shaped through a recognition-based culture in school and sports—there are a lot of "participation ribbons," as they say. It's not about winning or losing, it's about showing up and trying your best. That was the intended message.

Not being a millennial myself, I wonder what impact a recognition-based culture is having on this generation and the relationship to imposter syndrome. When people are being flippant, they say things like, "Millennials want to get a participation trophy for everything." While I don't personally believe that to be true, there has been a deliberate shift in our school norms to reward more people, not just "winners." We watched entire generations struggle with self-confidence and competition. To combat that and instill more self-confidence in our kids, we switched to lots of recognition and praise. Time will tell whether or not this will help people feel more confident and truly believe in themselves or if, like the example above related to Clance and Imes's research, this generation will instead start to suspect the praise and feel like imposters even more strongly.

The pressure to perform is real. Personally, in any role I've ever held, I've felt the need to deliver 110 percent above and beyond what was asked of me. I have a belief that if I go the extra mile, someone will notice my contributions. As such, this belief has set me up for situations where I'm disappointed in the result. I've recently come to appreciate that not everyone has that belief, particularly some of the men I know, and our conversations have been very eye-opening!

I was talking to a male counterpart of mine, Derek. I was telling him about something I needed to deliver for work, and I didn't believe it was the right solution. But since it was what was being asked, I tried to go above and beyond and offer an even better solution to the problem. Even though the client agreed it would be great to have the ice cream with the cherry on top, what they wanted was the basic solution. It required me to scale way back and deliver something that I knew would be a Band-Aid. I knew in my heart that the better solution was to fix the bigger issue.

Seeing systemic issues and patterns that many others don't see is one of my strengths. In this situation, I was told that I was overengineering the solution and to just deliver the basics. To do that required a skill set that is more tactical and not something I'm good at. Not only did I not feel good about what I was being asked to deliver because I knew it wasn't ultimately the best solution, I didn't feel good because what needed to get done wasn't something I was even good at. Even as I'm writing about this and replaying the situation in my mind, it's so clear to me that this scenario is a simple mismatch of skill to delivery. However, at the time I beat myself up over it.

In the moment, I was frustrated that the bigger picture wasn't being recognized. But more important, I was not the best person to deliver the basic solution. Instead of acknowledging that and just embracing that sometimes that is how the cookie crumbles, I beat myself up over not being good at that skill set. I should be able to be all things and deliver all things. I know that's not possible, but right then I couldn't get myself to believe that.

As I was venting to Derek, he said, "Why are you being so hard on yourself, T? I've always been OK with not delivering something that is well below my skill level or failing at basic shit—Einstein flunked high school math, you know. My parents always said, 'You are destined for bigger things.' And they were right." I was in awe. Because my parents also told me to believe in myself and that I could do anything I set my mind to. But their message to me was slightly different. They also said, be helpful; make things easy for people, and they will value and rely on you; and be a Swiss Army knife—it will create opportunities for you in the future. Go along to get along. It's these messages that set me up (sorry, Mom and Dad) to feel like a failure when I couldn't be all things to all situations. It made me feel I was an imposter because I couldn't even do the most basic things. I wished I could feel more like Derek, who said to me, "Fuck 'em . . . if they want someone with that skill set, let them go get someone with that skill set. You've got other important things to contribute." It makes me laugh now, but at the time I was not laughing, trust me.

Imagine what would be different if Blanche, the farmer's wife, had been encouraged to use her natural smarts and intuition about business to lead the family farm. Or, conversely, if Sara Blakely had been brought up in a family that did not encourage failure and bowed to traditional female gender expectations where it was more important to be accommodating, fit in, and not take risks. The outcomes of these two stories would be vastly different. The examples in this chapter show how the seeds of imposter syndrome are planted early and watered by our family and cultural rules.

If you are a Swiss Army knife but wish you could say "fuck 'em" more often, the Momentum section of the frAIMwork will help. In that section, you'll learn how to discern where the beliefs you hold about yourself come from and dismantle obsolete patterns created in childhood so you can replace them with updated, more empowering views of yourself and the world. But before you start building that momentum, we will dive into gender styles and assumptions at play in the next chapter.

Find Your Fierce Exercise: Journal about a time when you recall needing to fit in so you weren't cast out . . . or so you thought. What were the direct messages you received or more subtle signals? Describe the situation. Use as much detail as possible. Based on those messages, what actions did you take? Had the messages you received been different, what different actions might you have taken? Knowing what you know now, are there any different actions you would take to achieve your desired result?

4

GENDER STYLE AND ASSUMPTIONS

Working women still struggle with the societal rules they are supposed to follow to align themselves with any given culture's views on what is considered feminine. In the award-winning television show *The Marvelous Mrs. Maisel*, the main character goes so far as to get up before dawn and put on her makeup so her husband never sees her without her "face on." Women are still expected to do things to follow a given culture's assumptions of femininity—making everything look perfect while spinning a thousand plates in the air, with makeup on . . . in heels. You know, make it look easy!

Researchers have concluded that both men and women have felt imposter feelings at some point in their lives. An early study conducted by Gail Matthews at Dominican College in San Rafael, California, showed that 70 percent of the adults studied had experienced feelings of imposter syndrome. It appears that this experience doesn't discriminate and can happen regardless

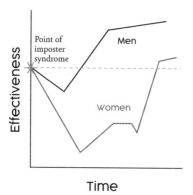

Effectiveness Dip

Point of imposter syndrome

Men

Women

Effectiveness

Time

of the level of success a person has achieved in any field. Men also experience feelings of self-doubt, but the systems they're a part of—particularly in traditional corporate America—are set up to enable them to quickly recover when it does pop up. In addition, being socialized as a female in American culture increases a person's chances of experiencing imposter syndrome.

In our culture, boys are socialized to be brave and to take risks. They practice failing from an early age and can shrug it off faster. Boys are also taught they need to hide their feelings. Girls are socialized to be well-behaved and to strive for perfection. They're not allowed to get angry. They're praised for good grades and for getting along with everyone. They learn early to fear failure and rejection. These differences in how boys and girls are socialized create big differences in how men and women approach their careers and how they deal with imposter feelings.

A DAY IN THE LIFE

An average day for many corporate women looks like this: She works extremely late hours to finish a high-stakes proposal. Then after she goes to bed, she stays up for most of the night in a whirlwind of anxious thoughts. The next morning, she wakes up exhausted after a night of little sleep. She spends extra time in the morning covering up the bags under her eyes. If she has children, she wakes them up and helps them get ready for school—homework done, backpacks packed, snacks ready. If she has pets, she feeds them, makes sure they have water, walks them, or delegates it to her partner or one of the kids.

Once the kids are off to school, she slips into her most well-tailored power suit for the presentation. She carefully modulates her reactions to the feedback so she is not seen as too aggressive because she knows that will have a negative impact on her message and possibly her career. After she nails the presentation, she races off to school to catch Junior in his play. On the way home, she picks up something tasty she'll whip up for dinner. She'll strive to be home before her partner to have something warm in the oven. Even if her partner is an equal contributor to the running of the household, she will often *feel* responsible for managing everything, even if it's just keeping track of what needs to be done. And she likes to please people and make things easier for them.

The messages women receive about how to be successful in society often drive imposter syndrome feelings. Women have long lived under this pressure to make things look effortless and easy; to not express feelings of anger; and to take care of everyone around them before caring for themselves. Remember the Secret deodorant commercial? Never let them see you sweat!

And even when she's tapped out and exhausted, she's expected to look fantastic, especially at work. A slightly disheveled man in the boardroom typically signals to others the long hours he's worked. He often conjures up sympathy from his coworkers since he never looks that ragged without a good, well-earned reason. Women often don't get the same grace—from others or themselves. Google "how to make things look effortless" and you will be rewarded with a barrage of links to articles geared toward women about how to look great, feel great, be great without making it look hard. Why is it bad for something to look like it was a challenge for us? A recent *Huffington Post* article focused on pressures of women in college outlined that "effortless perfection" is something driving many college women to "work a second shift in life," striving to not only get good grades but to be fit, pretty, friendly, approachable, and funny at the same time.

I was recently indulging in a guilty pleasure of reading *Us Weekly* magazine to decompress and catch up on all things in the world of celebrity gossip. I poured a glass of wine and dove in. It was fun. At least for a while. It quickly became clear that the magazine's focus was less about celebrity comings and goings and more about tearing people down. That's a lot less fun. Women in particular are targets in these tabloids.

As I read the magazine, every single page seemed to have something in it that talked about either a woman's weight, the plastic surgery she may (or may not) have had, or whether she was any good in her last film. The ads were geared toward weight loss pills, wrinkle creams, and scantily clad fashions. One particular story had a large picture of Britney Spears walking out of a Whole Foods. She was wearing shorts and a tank top, her hair was down in a casual way, and she had sunglasses on. The article said that Britney was clearly spiraling out of control again because she'd ventured out to the store and hadn't even cared what she was wearing or made an effort to style her hair or wear makeup. What a crime! She clearly needs an intervention. Sigh.

REAL STRENGTHS, REAL BIAS

Despite the fact that women deserve to be in any career they want, they feel isolated and begin to doubt their ability and themselves, especially in male-dominated careers. And let's be honest, that's still *most* senior roles in much of corporate America—despite the fact that women are earning more higher-education degrees than men.

Women are fighting against biases that impact their advancement. In 2013, Sheryl Sandberg and Rachel Thomas founded LeanIn.org, which is dedicated to women and helping them achieve their goals. In 2018, Lean In and McKinsey & Company published the *Women in the Workplace* report, which described what's called the performance bias. In the report, the authors say,

"Research shows that we tend to overestimate men's performance and underestimate women's. As a result, men are often hired and promoted based on their potential, while women are often hired and promoted based on their track record."

The problem with this is that potential is forward-looking: we take bets and put people in the big job and then see how it goes. Performance is backward-looking: they have to prove it first. This leads to bias if it goes unchecked, and one unintended consequence is that few women are selected for senior roles if they always have to prove it first.

There are fundamental differences between men and women in the workplace—from the language used, to the way problems are viewed and solved, to the roles they hold. This doesn't mean *all* women act a certain way or *all* men think a certain way, but a majority of people enact behaviors based on gender roles that appear to result in the startling difference we see between the numbers of women versus men at the top. And the lack of role models at the top of the house creates a systemic environment that triggers imposter syndrome.

As people climb the ladder, their capabilities and skills must fit what's needed at the next level. Women are typically strong managers and are also shown to have higher levels of EQ than men. EQ stands for emotional quotient, the ability to recognize one's own emotions and those of others and use emotional information to guide thinking and behaviors. It allows someone to manage and adjust their emotions to adapt to the environment they are in. People with higher levels of EQ also have a capacity to handle multiple complex details at once and create cohesive teams focused on teamwork.

This also explains why women make such great team leaders. Have you ever worked for a leader who is in it for themselves? They take, take, take, and you receive little in return. While there are certainly women out there who are in leadership positions who are takers—no question— many are givers. This is what I call an others-oriented leader.

What's important to know about others-oriented leaders is that they tend to be outwardly focused. This means they get a lot of their feedback, ideas, motivation, and self-worth from externally focused sources. What does this mean for someone suffering from imposter syndrome? Well, a lot.

If someone is experiencing imposter syndrome, they are chalking their experiences and successes up to luck, being in the right place at the right time, or being surrounded by a really great group of people that contributed to their success. While this very well might be true at times, it is also true that most successful women have worked really hard, contributed amazing ideas, and played an integral role in moving something forward. When you combine a woman's natural tendency to be others-oriented with an inability to "own" their successes and contributions, you can see the natural path toward feeling like an imposter. There is a difference between expressing humility and owning your successes.

Women tend to provide thoughtful communication approaches and are others-oriented. These qualities create strong managers. But are they the skills needed to be equally good leaders? The definition of what "good" looks like in leadership varies with each leadership model out there. However, most models agree on about 80 percent of what it takes to be a good leader. The models cite things like high emotional intelligence, courage, and vision as key skill sets.

Herminia Ibarra, a professor of organizational behavior at the London Business School, contends that vision—the ability to create long-range strategy—is generally believed to be the most critical leadership trait, and may be the primary thing that distinguishes leaders from managers. She studied the leadership skills of three thousand executives and included twenty-two thousand of the executives' peers, managers, and direct reports.

Women ranked highest in almost every single leadership quality except the critical trait of both having and communicating a vision. And regardless of what other qualifications a candidate for an executive role possessed, if there was a lack of vision (real or perceived), it often prevented advancement to that role. "People recognize that women are excellent managers, but leadership is the next frontier. Now women are stuck at the managerial glass ceiling," Ibarra stated.

What is particularly daunting about the findings of

the Ibarra study is women tend not to communicate as directly as men. They are typically more community oriented and inclusive, often seeking out others' perspectives and bringing those ideas into their own vision. This tendency to collaborate means that women are often perceived as not having a vision of their own. A recent *Financial Times* article highlights that traits typically seen as female, such as being courteous, accommodating, and collaborative, are not seen as being characteristic of strong leadership material. The article goes on to say that in 2015–2016, the communications industry in the UK undertook an initiative, the Great British Diversity Experiment. The results of the experiment found that teams with a top-down approach were less likely to generate ideas than teams led by a more collaborative approach.

If you aren't being aggressive and quick to speak your vision, other people may assume that you either must not have one or lack confidence in it. The flip side can also be true: when a woman is vocal about her vision and ideas, she runs the risk of being labeled "too pushy," "aggressive," or "not a team player." This side of the coin will be discussed in a later chapter. Ibarra's research showed young girls are taught to *not* be aggressive. They are often penalized if they speak up or act out too much. She believes that gender stereotypes like these can be "very dangerous." And I agree. They can certainly be dangerous to your career. The answer isn't to tell people to be something they are not. If you are collaborative and inclusive in your approach, that's fine. However, it's critical for organizations to be inclusive of all styles, so long as the result is just as excellent and compelling as a quick response.

IMPACT OF STYLE

In the early 2000s, at a critical stage in my career, I interviewed for a job with Capital One Financial. I had six years of work experience by then and a few promotions under my belt. The role was to sit on the leadership team of a small business unit, working directly with senior leaders of the company. I would also be leading a team of individuals indirectly and through influence. In traditional interview fashion, the hiring manager asked me questions about my skills, strengths, and resume gaps. He said, "Tell me about a time when . . ." I thought it was going extremely well. Then, about thirty minutes in, the interviewer said, "I have to stop you there. I honestly can't tell what *you* have done and what *you* would bring to this role."

I was stunned. What did he mean? I had just told him about all the shining examples of how my team had excelled under pressure and surpassed goals. How we had created value for the organization and captured tons of unrealized ROI. And how after we were done, we were asked to lead another large initiative for the enterprise. I thought it highlighted everything perfectly. What else did he expect from me?

He asked another question: "Can you tell me about a time when you had a disgruntled customer who was unsatisfied with something you delivered and you had to make it right? What did you do and how did you handle it?"

I started confidently answering, "Yes, great question. When we were faced with that exact same situation of a customer who was not happy with our solution—"

He stopped me. "There you go again, explaining what you and the team did, how you collectively reached a solution, et cetera, but you haven't been able to articulate what *you* specifically did to reach that resolution and how the team was better by having *you* on it."

I froze. I didn't feel comfortable taking credit for the work and results the team achieved. So I described how I was a team player. That I truly believed we achieved the results we did because of how well we worked together. Then I said that I was a very strong communicator and how that made the difference when it came time to present the solution to the client and illustrate our impact. I shared feedback I received in past performance reviews from my manager and peers about my background, strengths, and contributions. He seemed satisfied with the interview overall, and we wrapped up our conversation. I was fairly sure I didn't get the job.

To my surprise, he called about a week later and offered me the job. On the call, he said he almost decided against me as the final candidate because of what happened during the interview. He explained that I was not clear in articulating my accomplishments, and had he not probed further, he literally couldn't tell if I was qualified. He was brave enough to share that he would have extended the same courtesy to a man in this situation and wanted to fight his own bias, despite how uncomfortable he was with giving me that feedback.

This made me want to work there. Many people wouldn't have even been aware of their biases, let alone go out of their way to address them. He spent the extra time with me because he believed I was qualified, despite the way I was portraying myself. It was a big lesson: talking about your contributions and accomplishments isn't bragging or taking credit away from others. It's critical in helping people see your strengths.

The feelings of being an imposter often don't blossom until they're triggered by social situations, bias, or microinequities. In a *Huffington Post* interview, Joyce M. Roche, former CEO of Girls Inc. and author of *The Empress Has No Clothes,* said, "As I entered corporate America, I faced many unknowns. Being a woman of color in business at a time when very few women were in positions of power, I had to learn by trial and error how I was supposed to perform." Once imposter feelings are triggered, it drives certain actions. "This made me so afraid of being wrong or 'looking dumb' that I stayed quiet in meetings," Roche said.

Imposter syndrome can be exacerbated by a myriad of systemic factors—including embedded racism and sexism within our organizations. It runs deep and has a tremendous impact on anyone who is a member of an "other" group, which is any group that doesn't make up the majority. Diversity is critical for organizations to be successful, yet there's still a lack of women and people of color in the leadership of most US corporations. And even in organizations with increasing diversity, there's a lack of inclusion—just because people are getting invited to the table doesn't mean that they have a voice or sense of belonging.

DIVERSITY ‹ INCLUSION ‹ BELONGING

There was a time where the focus in many organizations was around diversity, particularly gender and ethnic diversity. The desire was to have more women and minorities in leadership positions and on teams. Why? Because it was the right thing to do. A lot has happened since those days in the 1980s, and people now have a really compelling "why" for having diverse teams and organizations.

Several years ago I was working for a large company and the head of diversity at the time wrote an article on the company's intranet about how the group he led was changing its name. It would no longer be called Global Diversity and Inclusion. It was now going to be called Global Inclusion and Diversity. You can probably imagine the backlash and eye rolls this was met with. Simply reordering the words in a group's name was hardly going to get us to achieve greater numbers of women and minorities where it mattered most. However, the justification for the name change was motivating and had a motivating rationale. He explained that simply having a diverse organization or team does not lead to an inclusive one, but having an inclusive environment naturally attracts diversity. This was revolutionary.

Making quotas or having a token woman at the table does not accomplish anything meaningful in the grand scheme of things. Yet really understanding what makes an environment inclusive so that it can foster diversity—of thought, gender, race—can feel mysterious and elusive. If these challenges were simple and easy to solve, we would have done it by now because we are smart people running large, complex global organizations. This is not simple and easy to solve.

An inclusive environment is simply not enough. Yes, an inclusive environment fosters a diverse environment. But more important than that, belonging is what will drive inclusiveness, which will drive diversity. When there is truly an even playing field, people from all walks of life feel included, like there is a place for them and they belong. When people feel like they belong and can see themselves being a part of that environment, then they bring their whole selves to the party, including their gender, race, sexual orientation, and diverse thoughts. It's a beautiful thing.

There is a saying that if diversity is being invited to the party, then inclusion is being asked to dance. I understand the analogy and support organizations that are trying to shift the thinking of their leaders to not only look at diversity but ensure their cultures are inclusive as well. That is commendable. But it's not enough. We are long past needing to be inclusive. The problem with stopping at inclusion is that it still implies that it's someone else's house. It sets a tone that you need to wait for someone to invite you to the party and then ask you to dance, someone who is in the majority. We need to move to true belonging in our cultures. There is no need to wait for an invitation because it's your house too. You and I belong there. It is ours—not yours or mine or theirs.

DIVERSITY ‹ **INCLUSION** ‹ **BELONGING**

PEOPLE OF COLOR AND
IMPOSTER SYNDROME

I was discussing this concept of belonging with a Black female entrepreneur I talked to for this book. Dara is the definition of fierce, blazing a trail in her field of book publishing. However, an interesting thing happened when I told her about the above concept— diversity < inclusion < belonging. We were chatting about imposter syndrome and the concept of truly belonging. When we got to the part about how she doesn't need to wait for an invitation because it's her party too, and that's the definition of true belonging, she fell completely silent. We were on the phone, so I wasn't able to see her face. After a moment, I asked if she was still there. Through tears Dara said, "Whoa, this just brought up a lot of stuff for me. I am the founder and CEO of my company, so I obviously feel that I'm building an organization that I feel I belong in. Yet I'm still in a traditionally white, male-dominated industry. So even though I'm writing the rules for my business and following my vision, there are so many days I feel that I still need to try to fit into that mold that a white man set decades ago regarding what is 'acceptable' in my field."

Here is someone who spends a good amount of her time involved in the conversation of inclusion and equality, so much so that this is a fundamental part of her vision for the organization she built and her life overall. Yet it was almost like a phantom limb—even when the limb is missing, you might still feel an itch. In this case, she has created an organization where everyone can belong, she is writing the rules, and she holds up the ideals of inclusion, but her brain is telling her that the phantom of exclusion and not belonging is there. Having this script running in the background of Dara's brain still tells her that she may need to wait for an invitation to the party.

When you look at the company internally, Dara has fought to build a culture of inclusion and belonging. When she looks externally, though, she still feels she has to "fit in," and when that happens she may not always feel authentically herself. This can lead to fraud feelings and bouts of imposter syndrome.

Corporate America still has a dominant-majority

makeup of its leadership ranks, and that majority is white, straight men. When you don't match that majority makeup, it immediately sets you up to be an outsider. Women of color intimately know what it's like to be different from the majority and feel the need to be twice as prepared as everyone else, which only adds to the imposter feelings. When you don't fit the majority profile, you don't have the luxury of affinity bias, and instead you have to work harder to prove your value and show that your uniqueness is a positive attribute rather than a negative one.

Tara Jaye Frank, speaker, business consultant, author of *Say Yes: A Woman's Guide to Advancing Her Professional Purpose*, and former vice president of multicultural strategy for Hallmark Cards, Inc., shared her personal perspectives with me when I interviewed her for this book. "I think for me and for many other women of color, imposter syndrome takes on a little bit of a different flavor," Frank said. "It's a very human thing to doubt our own competence or preparedness at different points. But in my work with leaders, I talk about the power core. Whoever is in leadership is the power core, and whatever that leadership profile is, the people who most resemble that leadership profile are the ones who are given access, insights, and interventions. The further removed you are from the power core, the less you benefit and the more you end up having to prove yourself because of the affinity bias. In other words, the more different you are, the more unsure people are about whether you can deliver."

Frank has worked with leadership teams in corporations of all sizes around diversity and inclusion, and she has watched women with incredible skills struggle. "Women of color don't necessarily come into the workplace with imposter syndrome, but by the time they had been in a company for a few years, their confidence was eroded," she said. "It was kind of beaten out of them in a way, because it didn't matter how good they were, how many degrees they had; they were still not getting the opportunities other people were getting. By the third or fourth time you're asked to prove yourself it gets really frustrating, because you notice that other people don't have to prove themselves. So often the white man will get an opportunity based on his potential, while a woman of color—even if she goes in feeling confident—will find herself having to prove herself. That continued questioning of your competence wears on you."

This is essentially a form of discrimination that emerged in data gathered in the *Women in the Workplace* 2018 study by Lean In and McKinsey & Company. They surveyed sixty-four thousand employees in 279 companies about their experiences at work. The results showed that all women face everyday discrimination and sexual harassment—and that women of color and lesbian women face even more biases and barriers to advancement. The report indicates "Women of color generally receive less support from managers than white women—and Black women receive the least support. Black women are far less likely to get help navigating organizational politics and balancing work and personal lives, and managers are less likely to promote their accomplishments."

The day-to-day challenges women of color face in corporate America create fertile soil for the feelings and behaviors associated with imposter syndrome to emerge. Frank often counsels women who are trying to get ahead that one of the most important things they can do for themselves is to create meaningful, authentic relationships with a diverse group of people. "It doesn't necessarily lead directly to advancement, but as you grow into new positions, it ensures that you'll always have people you can trust around you who have your back," she said. "If something goes awry in your career and people are questioning you for whatever reason, you'll always have people around you who can vouch for you. A lot of people of color in corporate environments don't develop those deep, trusting relationships, and then everything can start to unravel."

I was once working with a few employees who requested a leadership development program exclusively for people of color (POC). I was curious and asked to learn more. The consensus wasn't so much that they needed special content or different ways to learn the same things that their white counterparts were learning. It had to do with selection for the program. Essentially, they requested that I build a POC leadership program; then, instead of making a requirement for entry be that you have to be a "top performer" or "high potential," they requested that this program be for POCs who were rated as medium performers. I was perplexed. Upon more conversation, it wasn't because POCs weren't high performers or didn't have potential—it was because when we placed those requirements on program entry, they felt they were immediately disqualified. They were rated lower overall because their approach to problem-solving is fundamentally different from that of their assessors (typically white men). I understood the point being made but could not bring myself to fix the symptom and game the system; instead, I asked them to join me in changing the system. If faced with a similar situation, I'm not asking anyone to confirm or deny, but rather to simply become curious. If there is something that seems to be deeper at play, it's important to uncover the root cause and not build solutions around the symptom.

In the next section of the book, we will talk about the importance of surrounding yourself with that support network that will have your back when you need it. It's called your personal board of directors, and it will be a game changer for you.

Find Your Fierce Exercise: Pretend for a moment that you're in a job interview and someone has asked you about your accomplishments. If you're uncomfortable owning your success, what are some ways you could let others speak to your accomplishments? Think about awards you've received, assessments you may have taken that articulate your strengths, or the words people use to describe you. Reflect and journal about the stockpile of accomplishments that are external data points you've received about your strengths. Practice phrasing those successes in a way that would serve you in that interview scenario.

Here's an example: "My team recently awarded me the Golden Trumpet for innovation, which meant a lot to me. Here's why . . ." With this example, you are leveraging data to validate your successes while allowing others to toot your horn for you. For this exercise, after you've written down some of those phrases, read them out loud. Practice saying them conversationally so they sound and feel natural. Go ahead, brag a little. Doing this will help you practice voicing and owning your accomplishments.

5

CORPORATE CULTURE AND BLIND SPOTS

Corporate cultures send strong signals about what is expected to get ahead. Inadvertently, those signals aren't always consistent for different audiences. The more people struggle with feelings of being found out, the more I wonder if imposter syndrome is something inherent to one's personality. Or are our systems and organizational cultures set up in a way to subconsciously reinforce the feelings of self-doubt and anxiety, particularly in successful women?

Most organizations I've been a part of don't set out to send a signal that the rules of success are different for men and women. In fact, the opposite is true, in that they have made great efforts to say the playing field is level. However, this is where blind spots can show up in large systems and companies. A long-standing philosophical question is, *How can you solve an issue between two groups if one only sees it as a small issue while the other feels it's a large, ongoing problem?* We all have our own set of glasses through which we see and experience the world.

GOOD INTENTIONS

An article from the World Economic Forum in 2015 cites numerous pieces of research showing a disparity in the perception of gender equality progress in the workplace. One body of research stood out: it was by Catherine Fox, a financial journalist who has spent her entire career advocating for gender equality. The research asked male and female executives whether or not progress has been made toward women's empowerment and career progression. Results showed that 72 percent of male senior executives agreed with the statement that much progress has been made toward women's empowerment and career progression. Of the female executives surveyed, 71 percent disagreed with that statement. How can two groups view the same question and significance of an issue so differently?

It's simple: men are answering that question through the lens of effort, and women are answering it through the lens of outcomes. We have women's networks, pay equity reviews, diversity councils, conferences dedicated to shedding light on the topic and uncovering areas of disparity. As a man, the perception is that there is a lot of effort being dedicated to the topic, and therefore the perception of progress is there. But despite these efforts, women are still not seeing an acceptable level of actual progress. Effort is tremendously different from outcomes.

With women making up half the world's workforce and the majority of college graduates, they still only hold about a quarter of leadership roles and approximately 7 percent of CEO roles. That funnel is narrow and obvious;

therefore, it's hard to feel real progress has been made. This sends a signal that speaks volumes to women about their worth and promotability, regardless of whether the organization meant to send it or not.

Several years ago, I was on a team preparing for an all-employee meeting. We would hold these meetings about once every quarter, and they highlighted significant accomplishments, large bodies of work going on, progress against the strategy, and any important business updates. A person working on the agenda spoke up and pointed out that the only people who had been selected to speak at the meeting were white men. We all acknowledged that there was an opportunity to have more diversity on the panel. One of the male senior leaders who was working with us to prepare for the meeting explained that there was a good reason the people were selected to speak: it was because they were the people leading the work that was going to be talked about. As soon as he said that, I realized there was an inherent, systemic issue at play.

The reason white men were getting the airtime at the meeting was because they were the people selected to lead that work. If you don't have diversity in who is leading the work, you won't have diversity in who stands up to represent the work. Most people wouldn't have an issue with the individuals leading the work speaking about it. But what can cause discord is when the only people being picked to lead the work, and therefore talk about the work, and therefore receive recognition for the work, are white men. Knowing that work products yield better results when diverse groups of people contribute to and lead the work should make us all question whether we are getting the best outcomes of this work when it's so homogeneous.

Back to the all-employee meeting and the all-white, all-male speaker lineup. After events like that, feedback was always collected from the attendees. There was an overwhelming theme coursing through the feedback asking where all the women were. Whether we liked it or not, that one display sent a widespread signal to the audience about what work was most valuable and who was doing it in the company. This had a cost. In that moment, it didn't matter how many diversity networks we had or women's networking events. The real proof was in the actions taken and who was being selected for top-priority work and having a spotlight shown on them. Effort versus outcome.

Not only is feedback like that a tough pill to swallow, it can potentially have a negative role-modeling effect. These kinds of actions may lead women to not raise their hands for leadership positions. They don't see themselves in those roles, doing that work. When you see people like yourself leading important initiatives, having a positive light shone on them, and being valued for their work, you can visualize yourself up there on stage. A more recent World Economic Forum article stated that women in general often receive fewer important responsibilities and assignments that could lead to promotions. Catalyst, a global nonprofit focused on issues affecting women in business, issued similar findings in their series called *Good Intentions, Imperfect Execution*? In the report they state, "Large and visible projects, mission-critical roles, and international experiences are crucial 'hot jobs' that advance high potentials further and faster, but women get fewer of these critical experiences necessary to advance."

IMPOSTER SYNDROME AND EARLY CAREERS

In addition to executives, I've also had the privilege of working with lots of young, up-and-coming professionals. Many were female rising stars who were being groomed for bigger leadership positions. About fifteen years ago, Shveta and I worked together in the same department. Shveta had a few years of professional work experience under her belt when she joined our team. Like a lot of early-career professionals, she had questions about where her career would go. She was confident and felt she could do whatever she set her mind to, but wondered where her career would take her, how to excel, and how to get noticed and promoted. She also worried about the imbalance of men at the top of our company, and what that might mean for her as a woman and her chances of success. As a senior consultant in the department, she asked me to take on a mentoring role with her. During one of our many talks, I brought up some information about imposter syndrome, and she said it was a new concept to her and she hadn't experienced it. We moved on.

Our careers ultimately took us to different parts of the globe, but thanks to tools like Facebook and LinkedIn, we have stayed loosely connected. Shveta went on to other organizations, where she was promoted rapidly and experienced a great deal of success. After several years of climbing the corporate ladder, she reached out to me and asked if we could talk. I was excited to reconnect with this wonderful woman and hear about all her adventures and success.

The conversation did not disappoint. Shveta had gone on to accomplish amazing things throughout her career. She led large departments, contributed to leadership teams, set strategies, and influenced organizational cultures. As we talked, she explained that although she was experiencing success, a growing sense of struggle was building in her mind. "I'm feeling really uneasy. I'm at the level in my career that I always felt I could be, but now I worry the leaders have placed me here by mistake. Maybe I'm just faking it all and don't actually know what the heck I'm doing," she said.

I asked her if she thought it could be imposter syndrome at play. We talked for a bit, and she attributed the question to the recent writing by Sheryl Sandberg and several others who are prominent in the field of women's issues in the workplace. As we talked more, Shveta suddenly gasped. She had a rush of memories about when we discussed imposter syndrome all those years ago. She said, "With all due respect, at the time I thought you were talking about a trendy, buzzwordy topic. It didn't resonate with me right then. I thought it was a fleeting topic. I think I get it now!" Shveta was fully experiencing imposter syndrome and was at a loss for where it came from, why she had it, what she should do about it.

So what happened? Somewhere along the course of her years of progressing and demonstrating her capabilities, signals were sent to her that she was undeserving of that success. She was starting to wonder if she had just gotten lucky and if it would be a matter of time before someone found her out. The question remains whether imposter syndrome is something solely inherent in someone that rears its head after an achievement, or if our systems and cultures are set up in a way to unconsciously send messages and reinforce certain beliefs in women who are achieving success. Many women don't think imposter syndrome is a "thing" until they start progressing in their careers and achieving the success they set out to achieve; that's when they begin to worry they will get "found out."

POINT-OF-ACHIEVEMENT TRIGGER

People often ask when imposter syndrome is strongest for someone. You might think it would be strongest early in a career when there isn't a ton of knowledge or experience yet gained. That hasn't been my observation. The answer isn't cut and dried, but what I've observed and experienced personally is that imposter syndrome gains momentum as the stakes and expectations get higher.

Those pressures may be self-imposed, or they may be very real. Most people come into this world fierce. They are curious, try things, look silly, laugh, fall down, and get up. When we are young, we know that the world can't expect too much from us—we are just getting our sea legs! As we mature, we learn what feels good and what doesn't. We gravitate toward things that we like and that don't cause us pain.

Remember how Shveta was concerned at the beginning of her career because she didn't see anyone like herself at the top of the house? It's even harder to give yourself grace when you feel like you have to constantly prove yourself because you're different from the people you see experiencing success and leading the organization. When you don't fit the typical mold, you feel vulnerable because the expectations for what "good" looks like are built on a profile that's different from yours. One blind spot in corporate America is that the profile for success is still largely built from what it looks like for men to be successful, not necessarily people you identify with. This creates a vulnerability for diverse talent.

The *Women in the Workplace* report published annually by Lean In and McKinsey & Company has done a brilliant job illustrating and highlighting the challenges women face in the workplace. In their 2019 report, they explain that while over the past five years the number of women in senior leadership has grown, women continue to be underrepresented at every level as you move up the ladder.

Only one in five C-suite leaders is a woman, and only one in twenty-five is a woman of color. As of 2020, there are thirty-seven female CEOs of Fortune 500 companies, which is just over 7 percent of the total list. Only three of them are women of color, and none of them is African American or Latina. Women are also concentrated at the bottom of the list, which consists of smaller companies. Only seven women are Fortune 100 CEOs. And yet, according to the US Department of Labor, nearly 47 percent of the workforce is female.

Women in male-dominated fields are especially vulnerable to feeling like frauds because the issues driving imposter syndrome are interrelated and systemic in organizations. When you're surrounded by people who don't look like you, it breeds isolation, self-doubt, and additional pressure to perform. This pressure is even more acute for women of color. The Lean In and McKinsey & Company reports have found that women regularly experience discrimination and sexual harassment at the workplace, which only drives this sense of being an outsider even more.

A friend of mine, Angela, agreed to share her experiences with me for this book. Angela had never struggled with imposter syndrome until a job change triggered it. She began her career in the makeup and skincare industry at a prestige cosmetics company, where she worked for the first decade of her professional life. Angela estimated that approximately 84 percent of the organization was female. Women in senior leadership? Check. Women on the middle-management team? Check. Female direct reports? Check. Women were in the majority, holding spots on every team from finance to technology.

"These were my formative years in business," Angela said. "I worked in individual contributor roles and manager roles, and manager of manager roles. During that time, I was surrounded by strong, ambitious, motivated, and accomplished women. And we supported each other." It was an extremely strong and tight-knit community, so Angela felt safe. She fit in.

That psychological safety helped her stretch herself and develop her leadership style during those formative years she was at the company. She was given opportunities to try things, to fail, and to try again when the next opportunity came along. Angela thrived while leading and learning from a place of abundant support. She believed she belonged there. She believed she didn't need to prove herself or her value. "Who I am today was galvanized in the ten years I was there," Angela said. "I never saw anything wrong with being assertive or ambitious or vocal or direct or any of those things, because that's how everybody was."

Things changed when her husband took a new role with an out-of-town company, which required a move to a new city. Since she'd developed so many skills at the cosmetics company, she was comfortable and confident in making a move. She figured she had a ton of transferable skills, so she switched industries and joined a large agricultural company, where she took a role in leadership development. Angela was in that role for a couple of years, but she missed the commercial side of the business. She spent several years networking and trying to work an "in" with the business side of the company.

"I was repeatedly told I had a nontraditional career path, and it would be difficult to switch over to the business side of things," Angela said. This perplexed her. After all, she had ten years of direct commercial experience with a Fortune 500 Consumer Packaged Goods company. No, she hadn't spent years in agriculture, nor had she grown up on a farm, but she wasn't looking for an opportunity in farm operations. She was seeking a role in sales for one of the business units. Angela knew how to develop key customer relationships. She knew how to determine if a business was making money or losing money. She knew how to build partnerships with internal teams in supply chain and operations. And perhaps most important, Angela was a pro at building, engaging, and developing a strong and high-performing team. After three years of concerted effort, someone finally agreed to give her a chance, and she took a role as VP of sales.

Angela loved it at first. She used all her past knowledge, and sure enough, it paid off. She knew what she was doing, and her business results spoke for themselves. After about a year, it became clear that having several sponsors was critical to continuing to progress into significantly more challenging roles. She reached out to the two other female leaders at the company and asked if they would be her mentors. One said she didn't have the time. She explained that while she was completely open to working with Angela and helping her be successful, she was already mentoring several other up-and-coming women in the pipeline. The other woman agreed to mentor her but was particularly tough on Angela. She critiqued her work experience and let Angela know she would need to "prove that she could do it here" versus tapping the twenty years of experience she had building businesses and teams externally. Angela was never afraid of hard work; however, she didn't feel supported in her quest. She reflected that in that organization's culture, there were so few women in key leadership roles, and it didn't always seem that the women were supportive of each other. She found some of the female leaders to be her toughest critics. It was like the women viewed the world through a lens of scarcity since there were so few women in leadership roles—over 90 percent of the business unit leaders were men. This sense of scarcity created a big impact on the women's behavior toward each other. It shaped the company's culture.

Nevertheless, Angela persisted. She ended up getting a male mentor. He was supportive but broke the news to her that because her path was nontraditional and mostly comprised of external experiences, it would be extremely difficult to ascend into a business unit leader role in the company. Not because of her qualification or qualities, but because she didn't have thirty years of agriculture experience and didn't operate the same way that most of the other business leaders operated. In other words, she didn't run things like the men or have the exact same experiences they had.

After some time, Angela pursued career interests elsewhere; however, she noticed that the challenges associated with having few female leaders were consistent at her new company, as well. "In my new company, most of the leadership was men, but most of the producers were female; real powerhouses, huge revenue producers," Angela recalled. "Every time we got on our monthly call, the business leader would welcome all the men by name. 'Hi John. Hi Neil.' And then when all the women would sign on to the call, he would say, 'Are the ladies all here?' It wasn't blatant sexism, but it definitely created the feeling that we were outsiders. We didn't feel like we belonged in the same way the men did." Angela's story illustrated how corporate cultures develop an "in" group and an "out" group. We did it to each other in middle school, and we still do it to each other as adults.

Angela started to feel signals from the organization that no matter what she did, she couldn't really make up for lost time, nor would she ever operate the way the men did. These signals communicated to her that she was not enough. It wasn't overt. In fact, as we talked, she had to really reflect on her time there to unpack exactly why she felt like she didn't fit in. And when you work in an environment in which you feel like you don't fit in, it can trigger a sense of scarcity that leads to fear.

COMMUNAL APPROACH

While community-building is serving us well in terms of team performance and cooperation, you may be inadvertently trading your own power and individual leadership for the greater good. Without voicing your vision, you could be perceived as passive or weaker than a male peer, and this perception is embedded within corporate culture. These fundamental ways that men and women define what's "good" in a workplace culture are the systemic and unconscious triggers that fuel powerful feelings of self-doubt. Figuring out how to balance that and allow for both traits to shine is important, yet it can be difficult to be both powerful and communal.

In the workplace, we talk a lot about the fact that *how* someone gets results is as important, if not more important, than the results they get. We want teamwork and collaboration and a communal approach, but the reality is our systems reward, recognize, and measure against the results, not always how they were achieved. So when you're viewed as someone who brings your whole crew to the conversation instead of bringing forward the ideas yourself, this inadvertently suggests to leaders that you couldn't do it yourself. This puts a woman in a difficult position, because corporate cultures often view a more communal method as inefficient or passive.

Gender differences create a playbook of sorts that tell us what effectiveness looks like in the workplace. If the person making the determination of what "good" looks like is a man, which is often the case given they are in more senior roles, then a more dominant, fast approach to problem-solving is rewarded. When the dominant, fast approach is naturally demonstrated by other men, something simple like this leads to having more men in decision-making roles and the cycle, bias, and blind spots continue.

Yet if a woman does not act in a communal way and is too bold and independent, others view her negatively. Women leaders are constantly having to ask themselves, *The next time I have an idea, how do I pitch it, package it, and make it perfect in a way that allows my voice to be heard?* Knowing they're going to be graded differently than men drives overthinking and overpreparing and forces women to put on the mask they think will get them the most reward instead of following their instincts and natural abilities. When that mask goes on, it creates the perfect environment to begin second-guessing themselves, a classic indicator of imposter syndrome.

You met Emily earlier. When we met to do the interview for this book, we discussed in and out groups and barriers she has experienced. When Emily took a communications job in the tech field, she suddenly found herself in a strange land where people spoke a different language. "I didn't know what the heck they were talking about 90 percent of the time," she said. "I was in communications, so I was supposed to communicate about what the engineers were doing. They acted like I should already know what they were talking about, and I totally shut down. I was having near hyperventilating attacks before I'd go to work because I kept thinking, 'They're going to know I'm the wrong person for this job because I don't know if what they're saying is right or not. And I can't say I don't know.'"

Emily and the rest of the leadership team decided to unpack the barrier that language created between the engineers and the nontech people within the company. "It's a small, subtle thing, but the high-tech language created an in-group and an out-group at work," she said. "It was not leading us to an inclusive culture, and we talked about ways to change the environment so people wouldn't feel excluded. But the reality is, in a lot of corporate cultures this kind of exclusion is a blind spot unless someone is willing to speak up. Someone has to be willing to say, 'Hey, you're creating this environment, and this is why most people don't want to raise their hand to tell you they don't know what you're talking about.'" As Emily pointed out, someone had to be willing to stand up and speak up to make the organization more inclusive. This can be incredibly challenging when you consider that the rules of belonging are embedded not only in our language and biases, but even our dress codes.

SO MANY RULES

The corporate rules men follow don't always work for women. And these rules are often invisible—for instance, they can be embedded in places we don't think to look. It's funny that something as simple as a dress code can add fuel to the fire of imposter syndrome, yet it has played out time and time again. Every industry has its stated and unstated rules of engagement, including what someone needs to look like to fit in and play the part. Dress codes are an example of something that defines a company culture and gives people the opportunity to judge themselves and others against what is acceptable. Do any of these look familiar?

- No open-toed shoes or strappy sandals
- No bare shoulders or spaghetti-strap tops
- A skirt must be no less than two fingers' width above the knee

Notice these all apply to women. At some point a pro-verbial corporate uniform became the norm. You've seen it. A navy blue or brown suit, matching sensible shoes, and understated hair, makeup, and jewelry. This type of outfit became the expected uniform for women to fit in—especially in a male-dominated work world. Younger professionals are starting to push the envelope and change this, which is awesome, but people in senior leader roles still predominantly have ensured they fit in. Therefore, they perpetuate the rules of what it takes to fit in—which creates a homogeneous environment.

As more women entered the corporate world, they didn't want to be judged by their looks or attract sexual attention. They wanted to be noticed for their smarts, skills, and talents. As their presences became a more permanent and prominent fixture in offices across the United States, this corporate uniform helped women to fit in.

Enter the menswear-inspired power suits of the 1980s, complete with boxy cuts and big shoulder pads. When I began my career, I scraped my pennies together to overhaul my closet. It was filled with fun colors and accessories, but I moved those outfits aside to make room for the corporate uniform. The suits weren't cheap, but I believed they were the price of entry for success if I was going to climb the ladder.

While I was proud I could buy myself a few of these expensive power suits and have them tailored to fit, I didn't really feel powerful in them. They were uncomfortable and didn't make me feel like myself. In many ways, the dress code contributed to the feeling that I didn't belong. Still, I played the game. As I was recognized for my accomplishments with promotions and new roles, I continued to dress in the corporate uniform. I left more of my authentic preferences behind, creating a persona at work who didn't dress like me or reflect who I was. This division, though seemingly minor, is a window that imposter syndrome can squeeze through to derail feelings of true success. When you don't feel your best, you won't be your best. There is a cost to that.

I've observed many differences between men and women in the workplace, from language choice to speech patterns to problem-solving. Let's use problem-solving as an example. What I've observed is that men tend to converge their thinking by isolating the issue and clarifying the problem. Women tend to take a broader approach, looking at a wide array of possible factors. Women will solve problems by pulling people together and brainstorming outcomes. They will often rely on those people close to them and use discussion to strengthen relationships through the course of a difficult problem. Upon reaching a solution to the problem at hand, the purpose isn't necessarily for any one person to excel in the group, but rather to walk away with the best outcome and solution to the problem. When it's time to share the answer or make a recommendation for a path forward, women offer the floor to others, and in cases where they do speak up first, they often ask the group to chime in and add to their recommendations. Credit is given to the team, and if someone offers a unique idea, they are named and recognized for the contribution. Men will often ensure their ideas are heard and leveraged in the solution that is chosen. When working to solve a problem, they typically use less collaboration and instead brainstorm alone to come up with a solution. According to Dr. Susan Heitler, writing in *Psychology Today*, men tend to rush quickly to the finish line when deciding or solving a problem. Women will explore various aspects of a problem, which takes longer. Each is at risk of impatience with the other. Women will often include more detail in explaining the course to their decision, which can be misinterpreted by male peers as having taken longer or being less efficient, when that isn't necessarily the case.

Differences are what make the world go round and keep things interesting. However, when people are judged for those differences, it can make them feel isolated or like they don't belong. It also creates a divide between the experience that different people have in the workplace. Until you understand those blind spots, the need to change will not come to light.

Find Your Fierce Exercise: Reflect on blind spots you've seen in your past or current work environments. Have you ever fallen victim to such blind spots? What were the circumstances of the situation? What has prevented you from speaking up when you've noticed these things happening? I encourage you to find ways to raise these issues and shine a light on them for your organization or team, if you feel comfortable. Think about your job. Does it use a lot of acronyms or tech-speak, like the example in this chapter? If so, challenge yourself to be inclusive within your team, especially if someone is new to the group. If you are in a senior leadership position, what changes could you make to uncover and eliminate blind spots in your workplace?

6

THE COSTS
OF IMPOSTER
SYNDROME

So far we've discussed the complexities of imposter syndrome, including the various places it stems from and how it plays out, particularly for women. But in the big picture, who cares? Not to be harsh, but honestly, does it matter? It's definitely interesting water cooler fodder, but if it's been going on for a long time now, it may not be a true problem that needs to be solved. Sure, these situations create discomfort and frustration, but does it impact the bottom line? You bet. There are many costs to imposter syndrome that individuals and organizations alike are paying for, including slow progress toward the advancement of women and diversity in senior positions within corporate America.

ORGANIZATIONAL COSTS

Today, we're experiencing a sea change in attitudes toward

the treatment of women, but progress in workplace gender equality is moving far more slowly—so slowly that the Center for American Progress called women's professional advancement "a stalled revolution" in a 2017 report. In 2018, their report stated that although women held almost 52 percent of all management and professional-level jobs at the time, American women lagged substantially behind men in terms of their representation in leadership positions. The percentage of female CEOs at Fortune 500 companies has inched up to just over 7 percent in 2020 from under 5 percent five years ago. This is a gain but not enough progress overall. According to the National Center for Education Statistics, women recently earned nearly 60 percent of master's degrees (2016–2017 class) and represent 50.2 percent of the college-educated labor force yet are still, by and large, hitting a ceiling at middle management. This is by no means all due to imposter syndrome. But given some of the root causes and complexities of it, there is most certainly a thread and tie that is worth investigating further.

This inequity persists despite research showing that gender inclusivity drives bottom-line growth. Companies with more women at the executive and board levels perform better, according to the Peterson Institute for International Economics, a nonpartisan think tank. And, according to research from McKinsey & Company, organizations with stronger representation of women and minorities in executive positions outperform those with weaker executive representation.

One way for women to reach the executive board ranks is to pursue competent and capable mentoring from leaders in their organizations. However, Lean In and the online platform SurveyMonkey recently released data suggesting that the #MeToo movement is discouraging men, who are statistically more likely to be in leadership positions, from mentoring women. Long before #MeToo, white men received more mentorship than women, people of color, and gay men, which certainly contributes to the massive disparities seen at the executive level. When people are mentored and invested in, it drives a sense of belonging, and that belonging helps to fight any fraud feelings that show up as people are advancing in their careers.

PERSONAL COSTS

Beyond potential lost profits for an organization, imposter syndrome has the steepest price tag for the individuals who suffer from it. Growing up we were blessed with many things, but money was not one of them. When I became an adult and could buy things of my own, like nice candles, I would display them on shelves and countertops, but I wouldn't actually burn them. What if I used them up and couldn't afford to replace them? One day my boyfriend (now husband) lit one of my nice candles and I had a fit. I shrieked, "What are you doing? Why are you burning my nice candles?" He was confused—why would I spend money on these candles and then not use them? We talked about it, and this moment helped me learn why I sometimes don't "burn the candle" and what happens when I don't.

Scarcity versus abundance: When you don't burn the candle, you live in a mindset of scarcity. My habitual thought patterns had me thinking, *What if I can never afford another nice candle like that? What if I can't find that exact scent I loved so much?* In moments when scarcity thoughts are swirling in my mind, here are a few things I've learned to replace them with:

a) That's not true—you will be able to afford another nice candle.

b) What's the worst-case scenario if you can't buy another candle? You will have the wonderful memory of the candle and all the great associations that scent will create for you in the future.

When you operate from a place of scarcity, you are in a state of worry and stress. When you shift your thinking to focus on abundance, you will truly enjoy life's gifts, including what the "candle" has to offer you.

Surface-level experience: When you don't burn the candle, you only allow yourself to experience a shallow interaction with it. We do this with each other all the time. Humans want to connect on a deeper level, but in today's society many of us stay at arm's length from each other, never going beyond the surface in our conversations. In order to truly find your fierce, burn the candle. Go deep.

Short-changing potential: The candle was created to be burned and release its scent and evoke emotion in the person who purchased it. When you don't burn the candle, you spend good, hard-earned money on something that's intended to light a romantic dinner, create a relaxing moment, or envelope your space in divine fragrance. Without lighting it, the candle sits on a shelf collecting dust. This metaphor shows that by not burning the candle, it's not allowed to be used for its full intended purpose. When you are operating from a place of scarcity and not using all of your gifts, you're not fulfilling your purpose. This robs you and everyone around you of your full value.

These examples have a parallel with what happens in our lives when imposter syndrome heats up and has costs. When you feel like a fraud, you are operating from a place of scarcity. Instead of dreaming big and putting your bold ideas out there, you play it safe and avoid any issues. People only get to see the masked you, not the authentic you. That is interesting for a while, but as humans we seek deeper connections with people—flaws and all.

When people don't feel safe or like they belong, we miss out on their brilliance, and we don't get to leverage their innovative ideas and contributions. Perhaps they take themselves out of the running for important roles. We don't benefit from their many, many gifts.

PAYMENT DUE

It's not like imposter syndrome delivers a bill with

payment due on receipt. It's not usually sudden like that. It costs you over time. Similar to how you are charged interest on a credit card bill. Or, to use the example in a more positive frame, it's like investing early to benefit from the compounding benefits of interest earned. Similarly, the compounding costs of imposter syndrome are huge.

If you don't speak up, stand out, share your talents proactively, what happens? Maybe you miss a promotion. Maybe you don't get a raise. Maybe you aren't viewed as being as strong as you are at your job. When those opportunities are missed, time continues to go by. It isn't simply that you didn't get this one raise, it's that your bonus is based on a smaller salary now. Your next raise will be a percentage of your current base salary. You start to fall behind your peer group—that's very difficult to make up as time passes. The impact is compounded.

The compounding cost of not feeling 100 percent comfortable with your talents and being willing to advocate for yourself has a lasting impact on your career. That's why it's so important for you to understand what imposter syndrome is and the ways it holds you back, so you do something about it as soon as possible. That way time is on your side, and the costs of imposter syndrome won't compound negatively. It's time to invest in yourself and play the long game for success, which is why it's awesome that you're reading this book!

Marci, a former colleague of mine, had a highly successful career for over thirty years in corporate America serving in a variety of HR leadership roles. She led leadership development efforts, as well as coaching programs. After her own wake-up call, she decided to work as an independent consultant and executive coach who works with top-of-the-house executives to enable them to be their best. During an interview for the book, I asked Marci what she thought the cost of imposter syndrome is for people and organizations. Her response was enlightening. "People experience a lot less happiness, joy, creativity, fun, and balance in their whole lives when they're not their full authentic self," she said. "And they have more stress, frustration, fear, and despair. It's like they're on a hamster wheel running through the motions. When people do that, they don't take risks, they don't share their talents, and they miss opportunities. If I'm honest, I had that aha moment myself." Marci shared that the real cost of imposter syndrome to her was the wake-up call she needed.

Once she realized she was falling victim to these fraud feelings and allowing them to drive her actions, she saw that she wasn't giving her full self and in turn wasn't being valued to the level she deserved to be. She was compelled to change course. Marci said, "All of a sudden I realized it was time. I had so much to say and offer, I didn't want someone else or another system to tell me what I was worth. Plus, I don't want to work forever. At the time, I was thinking I only wanted to work for another five to seven years, and I knew I could have a significant impact. I ventured out on my own and started my consultancy. Now, it's completely different. Who knows how long I will work, because I love it. It's almost like I'm not working at all. And *not* taking risks is something I simply can't tolerate. Not taking risks is huge for me now. I simply can't afford that expense. My entire mindset has shifted!"

LIKE A THIEF IN THE NIGHT

You don't know what you're capable of until you try it, but many women hold themselves back. We tell ourselves all the reasons why things won't work because we're afraid of looking foolish or making a mistake. It's true what they say: you miss 100 percent of the shots you never take. If you're always worried about the what-ifs, you won't take bold steps to find out what's possible. What if your idea or perspective shifts the entire room? If you don't speak up, imposter syndrome has cost you an opportunity to not only change the course of the work in front of you, but how you are viewed and your life.

Please don't feel like this is all your fault. We are pre-conditioned to protect ourselves. It's an evolutionary risk mitigation strategy that our brains use to keep us safe. Ever hear of the tall poppy syndrome? It's a concept where the tall poppies that stick up too high get chopped down by the Weedwacker. With imposter syndrome you think, "Don't stick your neck out, because people will judge you." The truth is, people are going to judge you no matter what. Judgment is a human response. Knowing you will be judged, how can you stand in conviction about what you believe? Too often we judge our idea before we even put it into the world, telling ourselves that someone is going to say it's bad. By doing this, we give our power away to other people.

Imposter syndrome robs us of owning what is rightfully ours—the accolades, the promotions that we've earned through hard work, blood, sweat, and tears. It creates a voice in our heads that tells us something other than our effort got us there, and we often end up allowing other people to take credit for our accomplishments. Now that you know what imposter syndrome is and how it can impact your career, let's get into the many ways you can interrupt the cascade of imposter feelings when they start.

Here's the issue: As it's spelled out in the frAIMwork, you can be aware of imposter syndrome and understand intellectually what it costs you and your organization, yet you can still suffer from it. Being able to productively interrupt it is critical, and that is what this book is here to help you with.

Awareness is the first step. Now that you have a solid understanding of what imposter syndrome is, you can start to build your skill to fight the fraud and find your fierce. Where we go from here is like a fork in the road. It's not exactly a linear path. The reason for that is that one size doesn't fit all. Similarly, not all actions are needed for all situations. There are short-term strategies to help you cope in the moment, and there are longer-term strategies to retrain your brain and minimize the number of times imposter syndrome pops up for you. The short-term actions are what I call Interrupters. They are quick, in-the-moment tactics you can leverage to get yourself unstuck. The longer-term actions create Momentum, and to build that momentum requires important, deep work.

First things first: let's interrupt that fraud.

Find Your Fierce Exercise: Do you know how powerful and influential you are? Make a list of the people you personally know and interact with whom you respect. Have you ever influenced them to do something different? For those you have influenced, make note of the skills and tools you used to do that. Maybe it was your expertise, maybe it was your ability to sell an idea, or maybe it was that you helped them see the situation in a different way than they had been thinking about it. As you start to build this list, consider all the ways in which you are already powerful. What superpowers are you leaving unused on a daily basis? What actions can you take today to start sharing them more fully?

Furthermore, metaphorically speaking, what are the candles in your life you're not allowing yourself to burn? Do you hold back your ideas or only allow people to learn about your perspectives at a surface level for fear that they may not like what they hear? What are the areas of your life where you are viewing the world through a scarcity lens? What impact does that have on your life or the lives of those around you when you choose not to use your gifts?

PART TWO

INTERRUPTION

noun

in·ter·rup·tion | \ ˌin-tə-ˈrəp-shən

Definition of *interruption**

an act of interrupting something or someone or the state of being interrupted such as:

a) A stoppage or hindering of an activity for a time
b) A break in the continuity of something

*from Merriam-Webster Dictionary

7

THE POWER OF INTERRUPTION

The ability to interrupt something is powerful. When you interrupt someone who is talking, it completely stops their idea and can make them lose their thought. When you fix a pipe that has burst, you are literally stopping the flow of water from getting all over the floor. As the definition says, interruption stops or hinders an activity. You are interrupting the continuity of something. It sounds simple, but this is one of the most powerful tools when fighting the fraud feelings associated with imposter syndrome. Stop them and short-circuit the flow of the thoughts and feelings.

To interrupt is not a singular action. There are several things you can or might need to do in the moment when you start to feel like a fraud or an imposter. Some are simple and others are more complex. While talking with hundreds of people who experience imposter syndrome from time to time, I learned many shared things that helped them fight it. I've collected a wide variety of strategies to share with you in this next section for you to experiment with. What works for one person might not work for another. It's critical to find what works best for you to free yourself from the distorted self-view caused by imposter syndrome and truly see and own all your talents and strengths.

There is no silver bullet, but together we are going to explore a variety of ideas for you to fight the fraud and find your fierce. As you read about the suggestions, choose the ones that resonate with you. If you want to really push yourself, try a few strategies that make you a little uncomfortable. Keep in mind, ultimately your outcomes are shaped by what you do. And what you do is shaped by what you think and believe. To unpack this further, let's start with things you can do that are relatively easy. Pay attention to what helps you reduce the number of times you feel like a fraud so you can truly find your fierce.

Many times while writing this book, I had setbacks that made me think I had no business writing it. For example, at the beginning of the process, I knew that I needed to do interviews to gather wisdom and insights. My initial thought was that I didn't want to take up someone's time on something I'd barely even started to write. Imposter thoughts crept in: *I'm not an author. Why would someone take an hour to humor my questions? I should wait until I have something written* were things I heard over and over in my head. But this book wasn't going to write itself, and it needed to be as useful as possible to as many people as possible. That was going to come from smart, insightful people sharing their wisdom. So, I started. I conducted many, many interviews. But the first one did *not* go as planned.

I set up a Zoom call with a female CEO who agreed to be interviewed. The technology was tested a couple times beforehand, and everything was ready to go. The interview was scheduled for sixty minutes, but we ended up talking for nearly ninety minutes because there was so much richness in the wisdom she had to share. The stories, the emotion, the insights—all magical! To be genuinely present for the conversation, I listened and didn't take notes. At the end there was an overwhelming feeling of gratitude. This conversation had surpassed all expectations, and as we parted ways, I couldn't wait to conduct the next interview!

The next step was to transcribe the interview into content for the book, and it was then that I realized to my horror the technology had failed—there was no recording of the interview! It seemed impossible, but it was true. Blank stare. Frantically trying to figure out if there was some way to recover the file and get the interview back, I sent a help ticket to the Zoom support center. They tried everything, but the interview simply had not recorded. There was an update that had been pushed out at the exact moment the interview started, and as a result the recording function hadn't worked. While empathetic to my situation, there was nothing they could do. It was lost.

I grabbed paper and pen to try to write down the nuggets of wisdom she shared, but I came up short with only a handful of bullets filled largely with words strung together that didn't mean much. While I remembered the high-level points of the conversation, the magic wasn't there. I wasn't able to recreate much of the interview and would have to start over.

Through tears I said to my husband, "This is a sign I'm not even supposed to write this stupid book! It feels like whenever I try to make progress on this thing, I take one step forward and two steps back. Who did I think I was to tackle this, anyway? I'm not an author, I'm a failure."

After about an hour cooler heads prevailed, and I texted the person I interviewed and explained what happened. She understood, saying she'd had something similar happen to her before, and graciously offered to re-schedule. Feeling relieved, I took the afternoon off from writing or doing anything related to the book. On a walk, my husband asked, "What can you learn from this?" At first, I was furious—please do not lecture me about tech-nology and how I needed to learn it better! But that's not what he meant. He gently pointed out that perhaps my own imposter syndrome was rearing its ugly head.

He was right. At a high point of achievement (a great interview), when something didn't go as planned (tech-nology glitch), I let my thoughts torment me (*Who are you to think you could do this whole book-writing thing? You couldn't even get an interview to record*). Imposter syndrome started to knock me down. Perfect example.

I used the frAIMwork to interrupt the downward spi-ral and pull myself out of it. In the past, it would have taken me quite a while to recover from a moment like this. My imposter feelings would have shown up in my actions, and I would have found ways to avoid working on the book. I would have avoided doing another interview. I may have delayed taking action toward writing at all. Instead, I recognized what was happening (with a little help, which we all need; I'm going to talk about accepting help more in a bit), interrupted the flow of the negative thoughts that were driving my actions, and moved through it in about an hour. If you don't interrupt the fraud, it takes over. Seeing the situation realistically allows for the needed interruption to stop the negative spiral.

This experience is a perfect example of how you can put the frAIMwork into action. When my mind told me I didn't have any business writing a book, I simply asked myself over and over again, as many times as I needed to until my brain stopped telling me I was a fraud, "What if that's not true? Yes, it sucks that the technology failed, but it's not you that failed, it's the technology." It may sound silly, but it was like a broken record or a type of mantra: *What if that's not true? What if that's not true? What if that's not true?* until I believed it and got tired of asking the question. I rescheduled the interview, and it was epic!

8

INTERRUPT YOUR THOUGHTS

Now that we've illustrated the power of "interrupting," we can move to how this practice applies to the frAIMwork. You've become aware of your fraudulent thoughts—the negative perceptions and unsubstantiated fears. Now we can begin the work of interrupting those thoughts. It all begins deep inside the brain.

NEURAL PATHWAYS

You've probably heard the saying, "It's just like riding a bike." This phrase is in reference to the idea that the task at hand is something easy to remember—once you get on the bike, you'll "automatically" remember how to do it. This is because the process of riding a bike for most people has become "hardwired" into our brains. Decades ago, when brain research was initially pursued, scientists, researchers, and doctors compared the brain and its functioning to things they already observed and knew—machines; hence the term *hardwired*. Unfortunately, this type of labeling and thinking itself became nearly hardwired in the way that society (and researchers) began to look at our brains. It was believed that once we reached the age of approximately twenty-five, our brains were basically set in stone.

Recent research has proven that this is not, in fact, true. You *can* teach an old dog new tricks, so to speak, and you can learn new ways to interpret your surroundings and your brain's response to inputs. Where there were once hardwired "circuits," researchers now see plastics—still strong, and at times hard, but capable of change. Neural plasticity, first posited by psychologist William James in 1890 but only fully investigated in the 1960s, is the idea that our brains are malleable and continue to be shaped and altered by our experiences every day.

You might ask, what does this have to do with corporate structures and imposter syndrome? Well, to find your fierce, you first need to interrupt your fraud, and neural plasticity is a key to make that happen.

The neural pathways in our brain have been likened to hiking trails, with each hiker or "thought" matting down the grass and widening the path. The hiking trails, in this case, are made up of dendrites, and the more times a person pursues an action, the larger the number of dendrites that the brain assigns to build the "trail." As we complete a task again and again, the neurons in our brains communicate repetitively, becoming more efficient in the process. This causes some actions (e.g., riding a bike or reading) to become nearly automatic. This same pattern of trail-building happens with our thoughts and reactions as well. We have automatic ways of thinking about ourselves and our surroundings, and this is what I refer to as being on autopilot.

The good news is that just because we all have formed neural pathways throughout our lives, it does not mean that we have to live with those pathways forever. If we are willing to do the work, we can retrain our brains to experience a new level of "normal" about our thoughts. Some of that work can include mindfulness and meditation techniques, which we discuss in the Momentum section. In Dr. Rick Hanson's *Hardwiring Happiness*, the neuropsychologist explains that our brains are wired toward the negative, but there is a quick exercise to interrupt our neural pathways in the short term.

Find Your Fierce Exercise: When you experience something good in your day, spend ten to thirty seconds (that's all it takes!) to really tune in to the goodness in that experience. If someone stops you in the hall and tells you your presentation was great, sit with the compliment as you are walking to your next meeting and really think about it. Pay attention to your posture, your facial expression, the lightness you might feel in your step as you move toward the conference room. Focus on the gratitude you feel that someone took the time to share that with you. It doesn't take long or take anything away from your day, but the impact is profound. This allows you to focus on the sensations of the positive emotions. It also reinforces the unique contribution and impact you had. You, not anyone else. Absorb that experience so it starts to soak into your long-term memory.

NOTICE YOUR THINKING

GET OFF AUTOPILOT

The amazing thing about neural plasticity is it enables people to continually grow and learn over time. The frustrating side of neural plasticity is all of your old habits and learned ways of dealing with emotions and situations have become, at this point, automatic—you're on autopilot.

Being on autopilot is going through life and not having conscious awareness of what you're doing. As a society, we are on autopilot. Some of that stems from how busy we are. Families, friends, jobs, hobbies, kids, sports, volunteering, helping neighbors, finding time for fun. As a result, we are driven by anything that will make our super-hectic lives easier. Cell phones, apps, book summaries, and even autonomous driving vehicles are things we are relying on to help us with our crazy schedules and lives. We want the easy button. If a task can be completed in five minutes that would have historically taken three hours, sign me up! However, when things are easy or done for us, we think about them a lot less and multitask more. We're not fully present. Ever driven down the highway of life and suddenly realized you are about four exits down the road and don't remember the exits in between? Scary, but it happens all the time.

When you are not present to the task, you are not present to the thoughts associated with the task. It's why texting and driving is so dangerous. Our egos tell us that we can multitask and be fully present for each activity that is happening, like a computer that has the capability to apply the same energy to each open task box. Humans don't work that way.

Stanford University has conducted quite a bit of research on the topic of multitasking and whether humans can be as effective and productive doing multiple things at once versus doing a single thing at a time. The research found that people who have several streams of information flowing at them can't pay attention, recall information, or switch from one task to another as well as those people who were focusing on one thing at a time and were present to that task. Multitasking not only reduces your ability to perform, because the human brain can truly only focus on one thing at a time, but also has been found to lower your IQ and self-awareness.

If you've ever been in a conversation with someone who is checking their phone, you've probably noticed that you ask them a question and they nod along. They may add a word or two to the conversation, which gives the impression they are present, but it's brief and surface level. Then later on, when you reference the talk, they don't recall the conversation, or maybe they remember having it but don't remember the details. Their awareness is lowered, and the information didn't get through. It couldn't. They weren't present.

Let's bring this back to how being on autopilot and in a constant state of multitasking feeds feelings of being a fraud. Women get signals every day that they are the "glue" for their families, and they are the great multitaskers of the world. They can bring home the bacon *and* fry it up in a pan. We are taught that we can never give up; instead we should "lean in" more. That pressure adds up, and being in autopilot mode is like a coping mechanism—a survival strategy! The first step to interrupting your thoughts is to simply notice them.

When we multitask or go through the motions of something, information doesn't get through. Someone is standing in front of you telling you that you are amazing, but you're so busy fixing something that wasn't quite right that you don't hear it. Perhaps there are signals coming your way that you are doing a great job, but your brain is only able to focus on the one piece of information you received that said something wasn't good enough. For many women, that criticism gets fixated on and causes real problems.

Find Your Fierce Exercise: Try this—put the book down for a moment and sit with your thoughts. Have you eaten lately? If not, are you hungry? What about your latest project at work? Can you believe what happened in the last episode of (insert your favorite TV show here)? Okay—that's the easy stuff. Now, sit and think about your last performance review or conversation with a mentor who told you something that was hard to hear about your performance. How did those experiences make you feel? What was your reaction and thinking about those experiences? This is an important first step in disabling your autopilot.

STOP THE COMPARISON GAME

Belonging is a critical part of a human's psyche. We all need to feel accepted and that we belong in the groups we identify with. The problem comes when this need for belonging has a negative impact on our sense of self. One of the by-products of this need to belong is our impulse to compare ourselves with other people. With the rise of social media, this is a trap more and more of us fall into with great regularity and to the detriment of our happiness and well-being. We are inundated with social media every day. It's how we keep up with old friends, keep tabs on our kids, and communicate with our grandparents. It's like a script running in the background of our minds. If we don't tune in and decide how we want to interpret these messages, they can take you down a path of comparison and judgment.

When we have a colleague in a high-pressure job we want to impress, social comparison becomes even more acute. You may have experienced one or more of the following:

- You feel you have to say the right things, have the answers, and have a brilliant, innovative idea before you will speak up.

- You're nearly obsessed with making sure you dress, look, and act the part.

- You don't want to let others down, and it should look easy in the process.

- You're striving to prove to a parent, a boss, or a board of directors that you're good enough.

- You equate your performance with your self-worth.

- You're afraid of failing or making mistakes because it will prove that you don't belong and that it was a mistake to put you in that role.

- You're afraid of success because you'll stand out as different from everyone else, or perhaps worse yet, they'll then expect even greater things from you.

All these feelings can drive us to fear that at any moment the world is going to find out we're not as good as they think we are. "We need to belong. We need to feel accepted," says Margaret Wheatley, leadership guru and the author of *Who Do We Choose to Be?* "When we do belong, life is better, even healthier ... but as people become anxious to be accepted by the group, their personal values and behaviors are exchanged for more negative ones."

For women suffering from imposter syndrome, it's easy to feel like a fraud when you believe that no one knows the real you. If you've created a carefully curated version of yourself, then how can you accept compliments or own your success? It's much harder to believe you have value when you're hiding your true self.

Find Your Fierce Exercise: Think about all the things that feel authentically you. Grab a notebook and reflect on your personal and professional life. What gives you joy? What makes you feel like you're in the flow, doing what you love, using your gifts and talents? When do you feel the most you? What is it about these things that make you feel so good? Now, notice your reaction to social media. When you are scrolling through Facebook or Instagram and see people living their best lives (because you know that is the side that everyone puts out there, right?), how does it make you feel? Are you happy for them and move on, or do you feel a twinge of jealousy or inadequacy? It's important to notice and be mindful of these reactions. The comparison game robs us of joy. It's OK to take a break from social media. Press pause on the Insta; free yourself from Facebook. It will be there if and when you are ready to reengage! Finally, journal about how you can bring more of what feels best into more areas of your life and be unapologetic about who you are.

SHORT-CIRCUIT YOUR FRAUD THINKING

Besides being the astounding cinematic achievement of 1986—and some of Steve Guttenberg's best acting work, but I digress—short-circuit is the next step down the neural plasticity trail. Now that you have sat with your thoughts and habits, it is time to question them. During this step, we need to first focus on judgments and facts.

This is an important part of short-circuiting your previous way of internalizing circumstances. It is very possible that you can't change facts from the past. But if the current perception is not helping you, you very well might be able to change your judgment on the situation. This reassessment is an integral part of the Interruption stage of the frAIMwork.

FACTS VERSUS JUDGMENTS

You're in a meeting on a critical topic. Important, smart, successful leaders are seated at the table. Questions start coming up about something you presented, and the negative self-talk starts in your mind about how you don't belong there or people will find out you're not an expert on all the subjects being discussed. In this moment, it's imperative that you discern the difference between facts and judgments. A fact is something that is widely known to be consistent with objective reality and can be proven to be true with evidence. A judgment is the process of forming an opinion or evaluation by discerning and comparing sets of information. I'm here to tell you that the human brain is not always your friend when it comes to figuring out the difference between a fact and judgment.

One way to do this is to take a step back when the negative self-talk creeps in and practice thoughtful inquiry. Simply ask yourself, *What if that's not true?* This practice helps you name the feelings or experience you're having without overidentifying with it so you can put space between your thoughts and your emotions. Asking this question forces you to think of the polar opposite of what you're feeling in a way that turns on the prefrontal cortex of the brain, so you have access to your problem-solving mind. It also creates space for reflection, which is the powerful part that helps you get unstuck.

Learning how to interrupt negative thoughts by questioning them is important because our thoughts drive our behaviors, which drive our outcomes.

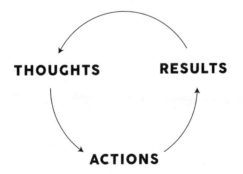

THOUGHTS   **RESULTS**

ACTIONS

If your thoughts are negative ones, your actions are going to be built on those negative thoughts. For example, let's say you've gained some weight over the last year or so but want to lose it. But you think to yourself, *I'm fat. I can't exercise, I'm too heavy and I haven't worked out in over a year* (thought). If you believe the negative thought that you are too fat and heavy people can't exercise, or that people who have not worked out in over a year can't start, your action will likely be no action. You aren't going to start working out; rather, you will sit on the couch most evenings drinking wine (action). That action will have you remain at the weight you are at, or possibly even gain more (result). Let's shift that thinking and see what happens.

You know you've gained some weight and want to lose it and think to yourself, *This extra weight I'm carrying around doesn't make me feel great, and I know it's not healthy for my future. I may not be able to jump right back into where I was previously, but if I start slow, I can build up my endurance and eventually be healthier, maybe even drop a little weight* (thought). You will take the first steps to try a workout that is suitable for your current fitness level, even if that is at a beginner's pace (action). Slowly, you will build up strength and be able to do more strenuous workouts and start to see the pounds fall away (result).

Beliefs come from a lot of places, but one significant source is feedback. Feedback can be direct or indirect. Direct feedback, like when someone tells you you're doing a good job or they don't like something, is easier to discern. Indirect feedback, like when you make a meal but your family doesn't eat it, is a little trickier. There could be a number of reasons why they didn't eat the food—maybe they weren't hungry. More than likely if everyone didn't want to eat it, it probably wasn't very good.

When I receive feedback, I try my best to see where it's coming from. That is easier said than done sometimes. Assuming the person giving the feedback is someone respected, I try to modify my behavior in alignment with the feedback that is being given. If that person is in a position of power, I usually feel compelled to take the feedback—they must know what they are talking about! Not everyone does this. Over time, I've learned that I was operating within a mental model that said I had to take feedback when it's given. But that's not the case.

Feedback is an observation and experience someone else is having. Part of the feedback may be fact and part of it may be judgment. Thinking you have to take all feedback given is not a healthy perspective. If you've ever felt that you need to listen to feedback and course correct when it was given to you (by a teacher, a boss, a parent, a coworker, a mentor, and so on), then this next section might resonate with you.

Find Your Fierce Exercise: Think of a situation where you were uncomfortable. Perhaps you were put on the spot or didn't like the way a conversation or meeting was going. This should be a situation when you felt you didn't belong or felt like an imposter in the moment. Write the storyline out. Consider who was there, what the situation was, how you felt, how you showed up. Now, go back through the story and note which parts of your recollection were facts and which parts were judgments. Once you know that, consider some questions you would ask someone else telling you this story. Write down your ahas and reflections. Here is an example:

Facts: You are a senior leader who is driving a significant part of the strategy. People are looking to you for your expertise and inputs. They may not always like what you say, but you are in that position for a reason.

Judgments: I am supposed to know all the answers in this role. If people don't like what I say, they are poking holes not because it's their job to do so, but because I'm a fraud. I don't belong here. I'm not as good as they think I am.

Inquiry: What if that's not true? What is the alternative?

Reflection: I may feel uncomfortable right now, but it isn't because I don't belong or don't deserve to be here. It's because these questions are tough, and they would be tough for anyone in this situation. This is the team's job, to poke holes and find the best solutions. It's important for us to answer them so that we feel comfortable proceeding as a leadership team.

YOU REALLY *ARE* AN EXPERT

Remember Marci from earlier in the book? She had so many great stories and perspectives she shared from her successful thirty-year career in human resources. She blazed trails on the topics of executive coaching, early career leadership development, and mindfulness practices in the workplace. Even so, she also experienced negative thought patterns that surprised her and needed to be interrupted. "I'm a very confident person," Marci said. "I'm always willing to go outside my comfort zone, especially when it comes to work. But there are at least two recent experiences that led me to question my own beliefs about myself. It's crazy that this happens over and over again and how important it is to stay in tune with it. If you don't, the negative thinking train will run you right over!" She shared the following anecdotes to illustrate her experiences.

An author writing a book on mindfulness in leadership contacted Marci for an interview. Since this was a topic Marci was passionate about, she was flattered and gladly agreed to talk. During the conversation, she realized the author viewed her as an expert, and it threw her for a loop. Yes, she knew extensive amounts of information on mindfulness and had something to offer on each of the questions asked of her, but she still didn't see herself as an expert—an authority. Marci said, "In my mind, I was helping out a colleague. If anything I could offer was useful, I was happy to contribute." By the end of that conversation, she acknowledged to herself, "I guess I *am* an expert in this area!" It was a revelation.

Within a short time after that experience, another person reached out to Marci for an informational interview. About five minutes into the conversation, she realized the woman was extremely nervous. "I wanted her to feel comfortable and to realize I'm just another person who isn't any better than her," Marci recalled. "I realized this person was holding me in higher regard than I viewed myself. This really made me pause. Here was another example I was living where I didn't see myself the way others did."

Marci wouldn't necessarily say she suffered from imposter syndrome, but hers is a great example of how our foundational belief systems drive our actions even when we're not conscious of them. Her story also called out times when she made a judgment about her expertise versus looking at the facts. She is, in fact, an expert on this topic. This misperception in our brains has a real implication because our thoughts drive our actions, and our actions drive our results. If you fundamentally believe you're not an expert or don't deserve the success you've achieved, your actions and the results you ultimately achieve will show it.

While there was not an immediate negative outcome of her not realizing early in the process that she was an expert, we don't know what this might have cost her. Perhaps the author would have asked her to partner with them, and she would have gone on to even greater fame and fortune! I'm making light of this here, but that is one of the more insidious parts of imposter syndrome: there isn't a way to know what might have been if you had put yourself out there and fully embraced your capabilities. As I've shared before, you will miss 100 percent of the shots you don't take. "What I consciously and unconsciously believe is what I hold to be true," Marci said. "I may not have gone after as many opportunities in the past because I didn't see myself as an expert or authority [but] rather someone who only wanted to do good work and be helpful if someone needed me."

Find Your Fierce Exercise: When is the last time you were hesitant to label yourself an expert, even though you have expertise and are good at things? Draw a line down the middle of a piece of paper. In one column, write your skills and areas of expertise. These could be things related to work (e.g., project management, leading a team, or giving presentations), and should also include personal skills (e.g., handling conflict, being organized, or time management). Make the list long and exhaustive. It might take a while to get going, but I promise once you start you will see you possess a lot of skills. Don't worry about how good you are at them yet, just list them. If it's a skill you have or perform, write it down.

In the other column, rate yourself on a scale of 1–4: 1 meaning your skill or knowledge of the subject is very low and 4 being very high. Don't judge yourself or agonize over this; simply rate yourself on each one.

Now, go back through the list and highlight all the areas that you rated yourself a 3 or a 4. These are your relatively high areas of expertise. One might even say you are an expert in those areas, yes? Keep this list. You're going to want to refer to it later.

FEEDBACK IS LIKE A COAT—
DECIDE IF IT FITS

Now that we've discerned the difference between facts and judgments and why it's so important to realize your expertise, it's time to assess feedback and determine which pieces are factual and that you want to internalize to take action on. You aren't required to accept all feedback if you don't want to, but at a minimum it's important to question your thoughts about the feedback and to pay attention to your reaction when you receive it.

Every piece of feedback is like a coat. Some coats are heavy, some are lightweight. Some are purple, some are white. Some are designed for certain activities, like sports or running. Others are too small or cut too generously. When a person or group gives you feedback or shoots down your idea or criticizes you in some way, try a technique I use that comes from the field of performance feedback.

Think of their ideas as coats or jackets that each person is throwing at you. You get to try on each coat and ask yourself, *Do I like this coat? Does it fit this situation? Do I respect the coat salesperson who is giving it to me?* You get to say yes or no, or "It's too heavy. The arms are too short. I like the color, but I'm going to find a slightly different cut in the same color." This mindset puts you in a place of empowerment. You don't have to stuff every coat into your closet. You can take the two or three that fit and that serve you. If you are triggered in a meeting and start to feel self-doubt because people are questioning your report or you don't have all the data points people are asking about, you can consider the coats they're tossing you and assess them for a good fit. If they fit, you can do something about them. This approach can help you take feedback less personally, which reduces the chance that you'll experience imposter feelings. It also allows you to move on quickly from any feedback that doesn't fit. If you don't agree with the feedback and you aren't compelled to act on it, don't dwell on it. Move on.

It is also super important to remember that even when feedback is 100 percent accurate and spot on, it's not defining you. It's calling out something you did or the impact you had. But that is quite different from who you are as a person. For example, when someone says a report you delivered wasn't helpful to them because they wanted it sooner or it was hard to read, you should first assess if that's accurate—does the coat fit? If it was late or was in a format that could have been more user friendly, OK, fine. Now you know for next time. However, it's easy to slip into a feeling that you were supposed to know how to do that report and that the feedback is telling you that you aren't a good report writer, or that you are not helpful. You must assess if that is true or if this one report could have been better. It's important to check that feedback every step of the way to see what is applicable and what it means to you.

Find Your Fierce Exercise: The next time you receive feedback, quickly do three things:

1) Assess if the feedback is a fact or a judgment.

2) Determine how you feel about the person giving you the feedback and if you are compelled to listen to it.

3) Decide if the feedback fits you and the situation at hand.

After that quick three-part analysis, take action on the feedback.

GET OFF THE RUMINATION HAMSTER WHEEL OF WORRY

Do you wake up in the middle of the night thinking about a mistake, a conversation, or a problem? Are you sometimes unable to turn off your thoughts and get back to sleep? If you had a meeting that didn't go well, do you think about it nonstop? This inability to turn off your thoughts is called rumination, and it can feel like you are one of those cute little hamsters running and running on their exercise wheel, except it's not getting them anywhere. Well, news flash: it's not getting you anywhere either. Yet we can hop on that wheel pretty easily and agonize over things. What's even more concerning is that research cited by the *Harvard Business Review* shows women are more likely than men to fall victim to rumination.

It's like your thoughts are on a train track, and once the negative thinking begins, they shoot right down that track. Our brains are wired toward the negative. If we have five distinct experiences in a day, four positive and one negative, the chances of us thinking about the negative experience before we go to bed at night are much higher than us reflecting on the positive. It's why there is so much research out there about positivity therapy and moments of gratitude. We need this positivity in our lives to break up the negative thought patterns that our brain is naturally gravitating toward.

Before my friend Jacquelyn had ever learned about the neuroplasticity of the brain, she was struggling with negative thinking in her own life. She and her family were in the middle of a tough situation, and she couldn't stop thinking about it. She told me a story about how she dealt with the negative self-talk and interrupted her brain patterns.

One day, while she was stuck on a track of negative thoughts, one of her stepdaughters walked in wearing a T-shirt with a sparkly sequined pineapple on it. Jacquelyn had the most ridiculous idea: What if she repeated *pineapple* to herself over and over again every time she started thinking negatively? Would the experiment get the train of her negative thoughts to jump the track to a different and more positive line of thinking? She knew she had to do something. She was making things worse by continuing to think such negative thoughts.

Later that week, while ruminating again, she shouted, "Pineapple, pineapple, pineapple!" It was so silly it made her laugh. And suddenly, there was a space that opened up between thought and reaction. Her body relaxed. She found she had more control over her thoughts and was able to make a choice to focus on something more positive.

This might be a funny example of how brain neuroplasticity works—silly, but powerful. It turns out, the more you practice interruptions like this, the more you train your brain to avoid negative rumination as often as possible.

Find Your Fierce Exercise: Think of a fun interruption you can create for yourself that will break the chain of ruminating thoughts. Experiment with this the next time you are in a swirl of negative or anxious thoughts. What is your "pineapple"?

9

INTERRUPT YOUR ACTIONS

In the last chapter, you'll recall I told you that the process of interrupting would take some work. After reading chapter 8, you can begin to envision this type of work and its importance. The reason that we need to do this work and interrupt your thoughts is simple: thoughts feed your actions, and actions lead to your results. We started at the beginning, deep in the brain, focusing on thoughts. Now it is time to move on to our actions and how to interrupt them.

PATTERNS OF ACTIONS

Zebras on the African Serengeti have a lot to worry about. From lions to drought to loss of habitat, our famously striped four-legged friends really have their plates full. Something taking up a much smaller portion of that plate is fly-borne diseases. Zebras, due to their noticeably short coats, are particularly susceptible to Africa's biting flies; these flies, in turn, carry diseases such as trypanosomiasis,

African horse sickness, and equine influenza. With a thin hide and lots of flies to deal with, what were the zebras—evolutionarily—to do? They developed a striped pattern on their coats that disorients flies, causing zebras to be bitten at a much lower rate.

There are many different theories out there regarding other reasons a zebra's pattern is the way it is. Some believe it served the zebras by allowing them to blend in as a community, creating a disorienting pattern that is confusing to predators. Others believe it was a herd mentality—if zebras are communal in approach, more will survive and thrive together. And still others think it has to do with allowing the zebra body to remain partially cool under the pressure of the Serengeti sun while also staying warm in the cold desert nights. The zebra is like a chameleon, blending and flexing to fit in, survive, and thrive in its habitat. The zebra's beautiful striped pattern has certainly served it well, and recent research in the development of artificial intelligence indicates that pattern recognition by humans has served us equally well. Human beings are pattern-recognition machines, and we developed this ability early in our evolutionary journey. In fact, recent research indicates that it is simply pattern recognition that forms the framework for intelligence. The more patterns a person can recognize and interpret, the higher the intelligence. Machines become "smarter" than humans once they're taught to recognize as many patterns on a chessboard as a chess grandmaster.

We humans are also pattern-*creating* machines. Ever

try going to your favorite gym the first week in January? The reason it is so packed is because all of America is working to create new patterns of activity, indeed, new habits. But just as a zebra would find it difficult to change its stripes, humans can find it just as difficult to change their patterns of actions. You have previously interrupted your thoughts—it's hard work, right?—but now it's time to continue the work and interrupt your actions. First, you must notice what you are doing.

NOTICE YOUR ACTIONS

UPTALKING

How you speak can undermine your impact. Uptalking is a learned speech pattern in which the speaker ends sentences in a tone that travels up so it sounds like a question. While uptalking may be simply annoying to the listener, this socialized speech habit has bigger ramifications. When you end your sentences in what sounds like a question, it can cause the listener to question the credibility of both the content and the speaker. It can send a signal that you're uncertain or lack confidence. This is a speech pattern I've observed in many settings, but I notice it most with women. When I hear it, I think that they are not quite sure what they are saying to be true. Or, that I might not like what they are saying and that they are willing to back down if I don't agree. That may not be true, but that is the impression I'm left with.

Hank Davis, professor and author of nine books, authored an article in *Psychology Today* about the topic of uptalking. He opens with a somewhat humorous story about uptalking and how in one of the courses he was teaching, students had to stand up and share the results of their research. The first person stood up and started.

"My name is Jennifer? My seminar today is on bystander apathy? There is quite a bit of research on this topic?"

Why all the questions, Jennifer? Just what is at issue here? Are you not sure of your name? Are you willing to change it if we don't nod our approval? Why are you unsure of your seminar topic? Does that, too, require our approval? Why can't you simply tell us, "My name is Jennifer and I'm going to talk about bystander apathy," and be done with it.

His frustration with listening to this intelligent person question herself so frequently solicited a chuckle from me when I was reading the article. Not only was his writing style funny, I realized I've been in that situation and felt that same emotion. It also made me laugh because I've caught myself in the uptalk pattern as well. But as the article went on, what was less funny was that Davis noticed this pattern across the women, who were presenting it far more frequently than the men. He further stated that softening of language and opinions through the use of questions is a way to not be viewed as impolite or too assertive. He asked, and I wonder as well, what is wrong with being assertive, and when did stating facts confidently and knowledgeably become impolite, particularly for women?

Like any habit, once it starts it's extremely hard to stop. Take stock in whether this is something you are doing.

Find Your Fierce Exercise: Spend the next week listening. Pay attention to when other women speak, and see if you can notice your colleagues uptalking. Then track the number of times you notice this speech pattern in yourself. Consciously attempt to break the habit by practicing. Try speaking with a tone that remains level or goes down at the end of the sentence instead of up. Ask someone to listen to you and give you feedback. It's a speech pattern that is going to keep coming up, especially if it is something you already do. It's going to take a little time to retrain yourself. Be patient but persistent.

APOLOGIZING

You bump into someone on the subway and say, "I'm sorry." You interrupt someone when they are talking and say, "I'm sorry." You want to share an idea in a meeting and before jumping in you say, "I'm sorry, I just wanted to offer up an idea here . . ." If you are in the wrong by bumping into someone or unintentionally interrupting them, the apology is warranted. But apologizing for jumping in and sharing an idea is unnecessary, yet so many women do this. Why do women feel such a strong need to apologize for sharing an idea?

If it seems like women are apologizing or saying they are sorry more frequently than men, it's because they are. Quite a bit of research exists calling out that women apologize far more often than men do. It isn't that men don't want to apologize or admit when they are wrong. Let's not make men out to be jerks or people who run around offending people and not taking accountability for their apology-worthy actions. Research shows that men simply have a higher threshold for what they think warrants an apology. And sharing an idea in a meeting is certainly not one of those scenarios.

An apology is often used by women as a way to break into a conversation. "I'm sorry, but before we move on, I wanted to say that I think it's important that we explore all of our options before moving forward with this decision." Instead of apologizing for jumping in on the conversation, she could simply say, "Before we move on, it's important that we explore all of our options . . ." It allows her to break in and contribute without the negative impact of apologizing for doing so. After all, she didn't do anything wrong.

Day in and day out, I observe people running from one meeting to another. It's very much the reality of corporate culture these days. It's not uncommon to be double- or triple-booked, trying to squeeze everything in. This can cause people to be late to the start of a meeting. My observation is that it is far more common for women to come screeching into a meeting, feeling flustered and apologizing profusely for being late. Overapologizing for this type of event, which is quite common for all people to experience, can be damaging to women. The solution is not to be rude or inconsiderate of other people's time. However, people should evaluate if the crime warrants the profuse apology that many women tend to offer up.

Find Your Fierce Exercise: Reflect on the last several weeks. Journal about situations when you apologized for something. If you can't come up with anything, for the next twenty-four hours take note of when you apologize and write the situation down in your journal. Now, review the situations. Practice rephrasing your apology using a positive redirection. For example, instead of saying, "I'm so sorry for running late," try "Thank you for waiting for me." Notice the reshifting of power and tone, which has a positive and powerful impact.

QUALIFYING

In an effort to change their communication style and appear softer or more agreeable, women diminish the impact of their ideas and their words. I've done it so many times, and it makes my blood boil when I am able to take a step back and notice it. Though more often than not, I don't notice it. It's part of the fabric of my communication style. For me, this will be a lifelong course correction, but I'm up for the task because it's so incredibly important.

Tara Mohr, author of *Playing Big*, does a fantastic job calling out the ineffective word choices and sentence fillers that women use as qualifiers to their main point. These little qualifying demons may seem like small things, but when women do them in their regular speech and email patterns, they add up to big problems. The reason they become problems is they minimize the impact a woman has because they come across as less confident and competent than they are. Several qualifiers that need to be removed from your vocabulary pronto are:

- Saying *actually* before your point. For example, "I actually don't agree with that" or "I actually would like to ask a question about this . . ." By saying *actually* in front of your statement or question, you sound surprised by your own question or statement.

- Saying *just* before your statements. For example, "I just wanted to send you an email to ask . . ." or "I just think we should do XYZ, instead . . ." It minimizes what you said or asked. What you are saying is important, so don't downplay it by saying *just* first.

- Inserting *qualifiers* into your sentence before your main point. For example, "You may have already thought of this, but . . ." or "I may be barking up the wrong tree here, but . . ." Doing this also undermines the importance of your contribution or opinion. If someone has already thought of the idea, they will tell you.

- Closing your statements with *questions*. For example, "Does this make sense?" or "Am I being clear? Maybe I'm not . . ." Women tend to do this as a way of softening their point of view after they state it in case someone doesn't understand or agree. It's also a signal that you are checking for understanding. However, it rarely lands well. It will either come across as condescending or imply that you were not being clear in your statement. Again, the listener will let you know if they have questions or need more clarification.

Why do we do this? For women, it's relatively simple: we are trying to avoid being labeled as one of the many unsavory descriptors that bestow our crew of women— labels like "bossy," "bitchy," "aggressive," or "masculine." (Heaven forbid!) It's an interesting phenomenon when people do this and is usually an unconscious speech pattern that takes some time to undo. You may not even be aware that you are doing it.

There are two options for how this section of the book

could be closed. See what you think as you read them both and what impact they have on you as a reader.

Option 1: So, in short, I guess I just wanted to say that you are awesome? And maybe you've already thought of this or someone has already told you this, and if so, just disregard what I'm saying, but you have the power to change the world. I might be barking up the wrong tree here, but I wanted to offer it to you as something to think about. If I'm incorrect, I'm sorry for taking up your time with this section of the book. Does that make sense?

Option 2: You are fierce, and you have the power to change the world. (By the way, I like your zebra stripes.)

Find Your Fierce Exercise: Open the last several emails you've sent, the longer the better. Scan the emails for words and phrases like *just, maybe, sort of, does that make sense?* and *actually*. Rewrite the email without those words and read it out loud to yourself. Do you notice a difference in the tone and the confidence that is portrayed? If you find that you are using these words frequently, you will need to scan your messages every time you send them for a while. This is a habit that is difficult to break, but it's well worth the effort.

SHORT-CIRCUIT YOUR FRAUD ACTIONS

PAUSING IS POWERFUL

The ability to hit the pause button is extremely important. It's like a tape recorder—if I need a moment to gather my thoughts before being interviewed for a podcast, I ask the interviewer to hit pause on the recording, breathe, and think about what I want to say. Pausing in your day-to-day life allows you to take control of a situation before reacting. You get to choose how you feel about something flying at you instead of taking it at face value. Pausing and slowing down is a great technique for getting out of the autopilot mode we talked about previously.

Oprah Winfrey has spoken extensively about the power of pausing and being with yourself. She has long studied the principles of meditation and how to quiet the mind. She makes sure to pause every morning to gain perspective. This allows her to be present, plan, and get her bearings. Like meditation, pausing isn't something you do once. In an article for Oprah.com, she said, "It's a sad and confusing predicament to be lost in the world—I know because I've experienced time and again what the disconnectedness feels like. You start believing what the world has to say about you, whether it's the world in your head or the world outside. That outside world is constantly trying to convince you you're not enough."

To fight the fraud and find your fierce, you need to be grounded in your own self-view. If the world outside is always trying to tell you you're not enough, you must pause and give yourself the gift of remembering that you are. While it isn't a one-and-done technique, pausing can be a quick and effective one.

Find Your Fierce Exercise: A pause can be five minutes to gather your thoughts and make a plan. It can be thirty seconds to take a deep breath and recenter yourself. It can be fifteen minutes to go for a walk to change your surroundings before diving back into the situation. The next time you are asked a question, before answering, give a pause. It may feel awkward at first, but to the listener, pauses are helpful. Pausing will give your listener a break, get them on the edge of their seat for what you are about to say, and give you a chance to collect your thoughts before speaking.

REFLECT ON YOUR FIERCENESS

Look at the evidence-based proof that you do belong, and you are fierce. Reflect on a success you recently had that you are proud of. If need be, dig out your resume. Look at the roles you've held and the results you've achieved so far. Not anyone could have done that! Sometimes I look at my own LinkedIn profile and reminisce about the jobs

I've held. I remember big decisions I had to make along the way. I think about the times I had to take a risk that paid off and reinforced exactly why I had the job. Get that app on your phone and look yourself up every now and again. This can be a fantastic strategy to interrupt negative thinking in the moment.

One way to start getting comfortable talking about your successes is to keep a running list of feedback and positive comments you've received. Remember my story in chapter 4 about how I almost didn't land a job because I was oblivious to the fact that I couldn't own my greatness during the interview? After that instance, I created a sub-folder in my email inbox titled "Kudos." When I receive an email that articulates one of my strengths or something I did that knocked it out of the park, I drag it over to that folder. At least once a month when I'm having a rough day or feel like I need a pick-me-up, I read through those emails. I do it for two reasons. First, it reminds me that I'm pretty darn great and add a ton of value, regardless of whether I'm having an off day. More important, it gives me language I can use to articulate my fierceness. They are words other people use to describe me, and I work that language into how I describe myself. After all, the words are honest and factual! Eventually, you'll become more comfortable talking about your accomplishments and successes, I promise. But this is a good place to start until you are naturally comfortable with it.

Find Your Fierce Exercise: Keep a list of kudos and compliments. It sounds simple, but this is particularly difficult for women. It can be hard to toot your own horn and not feel like a jerk. But you are amazing and have accomplished so many things, so you have to find a way to brag a little. Once you start to pay attention to what other people are saying about your fierceness, you will notice your strengths without someone even needing to tell you. Can you list a few things right now? Pause and congratulate yourself on your talents and success.

MOVE YOUR BODY

Your mind and body are intimately connected. When you feel tired, you likely don't feel much like moving. But if you pull on your walking shoes and get out in nature, within moments of feeling the fresh air on your face, your mood and energy increase and you most likely feel less tired. Moving your body promotes well-being. It can help you let go of tension and build your self-confidence.

Amy Cuddy, author of *Presence: Bringing Your Boldest Self to Your Biggest Challenges*, has one of the most-watched TED Talks of all time, describing the significance of body movement and body language shaping who you are. She is an expert on the subtle but powerful ways posture influences our thoughts and emotions. Cuddy has a famous example of posture called the Wonder Woman pose, where you stand up straight and put your hands on your hips, taking up as much space as you can. She explains that there is a psychological connection to the way we are positioning and moving our bodies and how we feel about ourselves. Being in an expansive posture like the Wonder Woman pose makes us feel powerful and in charge. Conversely, if we are slouched in our chairs or shrinking behind a desk, it sends a message to our brain that we are not in control; rather, we are weak or small. Cuddy's research also suggests that the act of walking and moving your body increases blood flow to your brain, which makes you feel more present and confident.

Awareness of the mind-body connection has existed for decades. In fact, there is a rapidly growing body of work called dance/movement therapy (DMT) that has been used to treat a wide variety of psychological issues. Several studies have shown that DMT increases relaxation and reduces anxiety in patients, helping them feel more in control and confident. This therapy has also been shown to improve concentration and attention. The more aware and in tune you are, the more you keep your negative thoughts in check.

The simple act of standing up in a meeting or shifting your posture when you feel uncomfortable helps you create a mindset shift so your next actions will be more productive and in alignment with who you really are (the person who has earned the seat at the table and belongs there). When feelings or thoughts of imposter syndrome pop up, standing up and physically moving your body will signal to your brain to take a break. Walk across the room, stand instead of sit, or sit up straighter in your chair. It's amazing what a little physical activity can do to shake you loose of that negative self-talk. It does the body good to redirect your energy from negative to positive.

Find Your Fierce Exercise: The next time you are in a meeting and something happens that makes you start to doubt yourself or feel like a fraud, suggest a short break to stretch your legs. If you aren't able to interrupt the meeting itself, take a restroom break. Get a glass of water. Break up the situation by physically moving around. While moving, remind yourself of the other possible (and more likely!) scenarios about what might be happening. Within a few minutes you will feel more centered and less consumed by that talk track going on in your mind.

PHONE A FRIEND

Several of the women interviewed for the book said that early career coaching and mentoring made a huge difference for them along their journey. The gift of having someone willing to show you what they see in you is invaluable.

During one of those interviews, one woman shared how she is naturally wired to think about other people and their needs. Colleen is a project manager for a technology company and had always looked for ways to add value to her team and the company. "I've always worked super hard and focused intensely on results throughout most of my career but especially at the beginning. I was taught that you should be humble and not try to take all the credit—who cares who gets the credit as long as the work was important and you get results?" she said. As she started managing others, Colleen said she knew it was important to get results in a very collaborative way, so she built a strong team. The team loved her and would do just about anything for her.

Colleen wasn't focused on getting recognized for her work, and she put the team first in most situations. She felt that while she was working hard, she also thought other people could achieve the same results if they set their mind to it. She didn't think there was anything particularly special about what she was doing. Luckily, her manager noticed the stellar results she was able to achieve with and through the strong team she had built. He took an interest in her continued development and started coaching her. He advocated for her with other senior leaders and gave her exposure and visibility to them, so they could experience her great work.

One day, Colleen's manager pointed out what he saw as her unique strengths. It surprised her. "I mean, some of the things he was saying . . . that's just how I'm wired. I guess I thought everyone worked that way and approached their teams the same way," she said. As she managed more people, she noticed that in fact, everyone did not think that way. Colleen noted, "At first it was frustrating. No matter how much coaching or feedback I gave to some of my team members, they couldn't rise to the occasion. Sometimes their work ethic was not strong. I started to see that my strengths and abilities were not something just anyone could do." She was taking her unique strengths for granted and didn't realize she brought a special value to the team and the organization.

Having her manager point it out to her made a huge difference and shifted her perspective. "I don't know if I would have ever noticed what I was doing that was special and valuable without my manager pointing it out to me. It was totally a subconscious thing. Once I saw it, I could take notice of it with others I was managing and more importantly for myself," Colleen said. After a while, that same manager approached her about considering more senior leadership roles. It wasn't until that nudge, when her manager held up the mirror for her, that she started to see in herself what they saw in her. It was a game-changing gift she'd been given.

Once Colleen knew how her special set of skills benefited the team, her leaders, and the company, she could see all the places the organization could use more of her unique strengths to drive business. All of a sudden, she realized she did have aspirations for bigger and more significant roles.

Imposter syndrome makes us believe that if something comes naturally to us, it must be easy for other people. Having a mentor can help you realize what your natural strengths and skills are so you can better understand your impact on other people and your organization. This sense of knowing can keep feelings of self-doubt at bay and also allow you to open up to other possibilities for yourself.

Find Your Fierce Exercise: Seek out a mentor for yourself. If you are a woman, don't only look for other women who can mentor you. While it's natural to gravitate toward those people you are most similar to and comfortable with, remember big growth happens outside of your comfort zone. Men mentor other up-and-coming men without thinking about it. It's a normal course of action. Find some male mentors to learn from and talk about this topic with.

PRACTICE SELF-COMPASSION

Compassion is the ability to feel and show empathy, love, and concern to people who are in a difficult situation. Self-compassion is the ability to extend that same empathy and acceptance to yourself, particularly in the face of failure. Many people are extremely compassionate when it comes to others but have a much harder time giving themselves that same grace without feeling self-indulgent or like they are throwing themselves the ultimate pity party. For high-achieving women who have a strong voice in their head constantly critiquing their performance, the very concept of self-compassion can feel soft, weak, or even dangerous.

More than one woman has said something to me along the lines of *If I am kind to myself, I will just end up sitting on the couch eating chocolate all day and not get anything done!* That negative self-talk places self-compassion into the realm of overindulgence. When people do that, they are viewing the concept of self-compassion as black or white, good or bad. Self-compassion is a continuum. At times it may involve sitting on the couch eating chocolate, and that is just fine. More times than not, it involves reflection, learning, taking a walk, carving out time for a run, or talking with a good friend. These are things that feed the soul and allow you to recharge your batteries. We do these things so that we can be more productive later. This is a mindset shift many of us need to learn and embrace. Most important, self-compassion involves giving yourself grace to accept less than perfection.

In the past few years, researchers have shown that self-compassion can dramatically impact mental, emotional, and physical well-being. This psychological tool is particularly useful for those suffering from imposter syndrome. Kristin Neff, PhD, associate professor in human development at the University of Texas in Austin and the author of *Self-Compassion: The Proven Power of Being Kind to Yourself,* has been studying self-compassion for more than a decade. As Neff says,

Why is self-compassion a more effective motivator than self-criticism? Because its driving force is love and not fear. Love allows us to feel confident and secure (in part by pumping up our oxytocin), while fear makes us feel insecure and jittery (sending our amygdala into overdrive and flooding our systems with cortisol). When we trust ourselves to be understanding and compassionate when we fail, we won't cause ourselves unnecessary stress and anxiety.

Neff discovered that self-compassion is made up of three core components:

- **Self-kindness:** Being kind to yourself rather than judgmental.

- **Common Humanity:** Recognizing that all humans are imperfect, fail, and make mistakes. Seeing your experiences as part of the larger human experience instead of separating or isolating.

- **Mindfulness:** Being aware of your present experience in a balanced manner rather than overidentifying with the negative aspects of your life.

Self-compassion helps you fight the fraud by ensuring you are at your best and not belittling yourself. Believing you are not enough or talking down to yourself takes a toll. If you don't change that perspective, you will exhaust yourself and perpetuate any feelings you may have that you aren't good enough or don't belong. Personally, self-compassion is an area of ongoing development for me. In true imposter syndrome form, I would beat myself up for mistakes or agonize over situations that didn't go as planned. I would hop right on that rumination hamster wheel and take myself down the track of second-guessing and wishing I could change something that happened in the past. When I notice I am doing that to myself, I imagine a friend just called to vent about what happened. I think about how I would demonstrate compassion for them in the moment, including what I would say to reassure them. Once I have that in my mind, I look in the mirror and say it directly to myself.

Yes, sometimes I feel a bit like the Stuart Smalley character from *Saturday Night Live*, but it really does work. It allows me to work through and solve the issue for someone else first, then apply it to myself. After all, in the words of Stuart Smalley himself, I'm good enough, I'm smart enough, and doggone it, people like me.

Find Your Fierce Exercise: While practicing self-compassion is a muscle that can take a while to build if you don't yet have it, there are some things you can do in the moment to be as compassionate to yourself as you would be to others. When you notice you are beating yourself up over something, imagine you are talking to someone—anyone—else. Picture them standing in front of you, looking you in the eyes, and listening to what you are saying. Imagine those messages are meant for someone else. Maybe you weren't perfect and screwed up. That's OK. How would you want to deliver that message to someone you care about and genuinely want to improve? Chances are you would choose different language. You would give that person a break. You may not have even noticed the mistake or issue that made you feel like you were a failure. Be kind to yourself. Change your tone.

10

ORGANIZATIONS NEED INTERRUPTING TOO

Interrupting imposter syndrome patterns requires the whole system to work. This isn't simply about telling someone not to feel like a fraud. If it were that easy, we would have done it by now. We aren't dummies. It's much more about becoming aware of how imposter syndrome shows up and what feeds it. This interruption of patterns is something organizations can benefit from as well.

REFERENCE WHO?

Organizational systems are typically built from the standpoint of, and for, the "reference man." The reference man is a concept originally created in 1975 within the medical field to determine the appropriate dosages of medications based on an average body composition. Through the years, the concept has also been used for many other applications other than medicine. It is similar to a persona. While it's called reference man, in truth it could be anyone, not only men. It was called reference man because the earliest examples of this persona-type development had a man in mind, as noted in the International Commission on Radiological Protection:

> Reference man is defined as being between 20–30 years of age, weighing 70 kg, is 170 cm in height, and lives in a climate with an average temperature of 10 to 20 degrees C. He is a Caucasian and is a Western European or North American in habitat and custom.

Even while writing this book, I was asked to think about who my reader was, including their gender identity, what type of work they do, where they live, what they are reading, and what questions they have that haven't been answered. I was asked to think of my own "reference man."

Companies think in terms of what their customer wants and how they act, and then they build solutions or services to meet their needs. As a result, products are also built in a way that uses a reference man or persona to speed up prototyping and time to market. Without question, this drives efficiencies. But it can also create blind spots and biases.

Google Maps, for example, was designed with a reference man in mind to help people find the most direct route from point A to point B. It evolved to help people avoid traffic jams and real-time accidents. It further evolved to help you in different modes of transport, from walking to biking, to public transit. I could not live without my Google Maps! However, when I'm traveling in a city I don't know or it's later at night, as a woman often traveling alone, I would like to know the safest routes, the best lit, the most populated. I've talked to many friends about this; for the most part, it's not something that really entered the minds of my male friends, but it's on almost every one of my female friends' wish lists for a map app.

There is a startling statistic that indicates women are 27 percent less likely to receive help in a public situation that requires CPR. When research was conducted as to why this is the case, it was found to be because CPR is exclusively taught on a mannequin or dummy that is anatomically shaped like a male. A very fit male, at that. People cited they were unclear on how to administer chest compressions on women with breasts. That level of discomfort leads to people not receiving life-saving care in a time of need.

One other example is autonomous driving vehicles. Research from the Georgia Institute of Technology found that dark-skinned people are at a higher risk of being struck by the vehicles because they were programmed with a reference man in mind. In that case, the reference man was lighter skinned. The computer does not always recognize darker-skinned people as an object to avoid. These are only some of the extreme examples of how well-intended, technology-advancing ideas that will make our lives easier and better in the future may have bias built into them because of their inherent blind spots.

The challenge in many corporate cultures is that the system was built on a reference point for a majority in business. As discussed earlier, that point of reference, particularly by leadership standards, is still predominantly white men. When systems are built with a reference point that does not help everyone feel like they belong, it fuels feelings of low psychological safety and feeds imposter syndrome, most notably for anyone who is a member of an "other" group. In corporate America, that is anyone who is not a white male, especially if the system has these types of blind spots. Unfortunately, many organizations do.

MICROINEQUITIES, UNCONSCIOUS BIAS, AND IMPOSTER SYNDROME

In the early 1970s, Mary Rowe, who was at the time an ombudsman at MIT and later became an adjunct professor of negotiation and conflict management at the MIT Sloan School of Management, created the term *microinequities* to define the subtle but systematic behaviors that often unintentionally create discrimination. In an interview with *The Institute for Work & Employment Research*, Rowe described microinequities and why they are so hard to uncover. "I believe that there is a whole spectrum of microinequities. These injurious actions range from microaggressions that are hostile, to inequities arising from unconscious bias, to those that arise from negligence, to those that come from just 'not knowing what one needs to know about' other people—that is, from 'innocent ignorance,'" Rowe said. Microinequities are small behaviors or gestures that signal an implicit bias. For example, consistently mispronouncing someone's name and not bothering to learn the correct way to say it. Interrupting someone midsentence. Only making eye contact with men when there are both women and men present in the room. Checking your phone and not making eye contact when someone is speaking to you. One-off they may seem insignificant, but together they have a large cumulative effect. Research has shown that when microinequities go unchecked, they can result in hostile work environments, but it's often difficult for the person experiencing them to articulate why it's such an issue because they are subtle.

Unconscious bias is a term used to describe inherent bias we all have as human beings that is deep in our subconscious. It takes many different forms, from *affinity* bias, where you are drawn to those people and things that are similar to you; to *conformity* bias, where people tend to act like others around them regardless of their own personal beliefs; to the *recency* bias, where you judge someone not on your total experience of them but rather on your most recent experience. So you can see that unconscious bias is complex. Unconscious bias takes on many other relatively self-explanatory forms as well, such as beauty bias, age bias, weight bias, name bias, and even height bias. We may not be setting out to be biased against or for something or someone, but because of our preferences, experiences, and beliefs, we are biased. To be biased does not make us bad, it makes us human. That said, if you don't work to uncover your unconscious biases and ensure they are not influencing critical decision-making, then you could be contributing to issues of discrimination whether you intend to or not.

Several years back, I attended a leadership development workshop where teams of up-and-coming leaders were assembled to work on a business challenge together for about six weeks and then present their findings to a panel of executives for feedback. An interesting thing happened while one of the teams was presenting. It was a diverse team made up of white men, a Black woman, an older Indian man, and a white woman, all in the "corporate uniform" of black or blue suits, all profoundly serious.

One of the white men, Paul, got up to present. He was a tall, fortysomething person wearing a well-tailored suit. His approach was dry and certainly all business. He walked across the stage, nodding toward the executives in the first row who would be evaluating him. He looked confident and in his element. When he went to present his portion of the results, though, he completely blanked. I mean, deer in the headlights, stumbling and fumbling, not a coherent thought coming out of him. He made a nervous joke and exited stage left. I felt for him. It's happened to us all. I have no doubt he was prepared, but in that final hour, he messed it up.

Two more people presented without any issue before Monique, a short Black woman who was about thirty-five years old. I had seen Monique at work previously, and she was typically dressed in vibrant colors, stretchy skirts, and flowing sweaters, always very polished and put together. That day, she wore the assumed-requisite navy-blue suit. Her suit was not tailored exactly for her body shape, and it appeared to me that she was not feeling super comfortable about her required attire for this event. She had a lot of hair, and for the presentation, she chose to wear it down in a traditional loose curl with about half of it covering a portion of her face. She walked across the stage, presented her facts and findings accurately, maintained eye contact with all the executives, and nailed the presentation.

Afterward, the executives convened to discuss the presentation and presenters. An interesting thing happened: while each presenter was discussed, the executives spent most of their time on Paul and Monique. They discussed how painful it was to see Paul struggle with his presentation. They agreed he was smart, evoked feelings of confidence, and must have known his stuff, but obviously had an off day. They went back and forth on whether or not they should even say anything about it, given that he clearly must have known, and they didn't want to make him feel bad. All gave him the benefit of the doubt and scored him quite liberally on the final evaluation.

When they discussed Monique, they agreed she knew

her information quite well. But they critiqued her clothes, her stance, her hair, the fact that while she maintained eye contact they couldn't really tell because of the hair covering her face. They commented on how she must have felt uncomfortable or out of place, because it showed in her posture and presence on the stage. They gave her a middle-of-the-road score and the feedback was robust, suggesting all the possible tweaks she could make to be even more effective.

I was in awe. It was clear to me that at least three things were at play: microinequities, unconscious bias, and imposter syndrome.

There is a significant cost to this scenario—for Monique, for Paul, for the executive panel, and for the organization. This kind of behavior fuels the fire of imposter syndrome. We are continuing to create environments that feed the imposter feelings. You must fit in, and if you don't, you have to "dress the part." And when that doesn't feel authentic, it further sparks those imposter feelings. This does not bring out the best in people.

Shifting gears a bit from corporate America to politics, I recently read a *New York Times* article that I thought nicely illustrated the unconscious bias women face. It is not uncommon for women in the US Senate to suffer from cases of mistaken identity. The story explained that when Senator Amy Klobuchar arrived in the Senate in 2007 representing the state of Minnesota, she stepped onto a senators-only elevator, only to be confronted by a male colleague. "This is a senators-only elevator," she recalled him telling her. "I looked at him and said, 'And who are you? I *am* a senator.'" The same article described how Heidi Heitkamp, a former senator from North Dakota who arrived in the Senate in 2013, recalled trying to step onto the subway that connects Senate office buildings to the Capitol. A guard asked for her identification, which she produced. "So, you're a Senate spouse?" he asked her. "No. I am *the* United States senator from my state," she said. While these examples are dated, they paint a picture of the inherent bias that still exists today.

And it isn't only men who have unconscious bias toward women. While writing this book, I received an email from a female in my network. She doesn't know me very well, but she was asking if we could connect to discuss an upcoming event. In the email she said, "Please ask your admin to reach out and have her suggest a time that will work for you." I had to read it a few times. Who was the "her" she was referring to? Then I realized that the assumption was that my admin was a woman. While it is true that most administrative assistants are women, this was a blind spot assumption. But in this case another female was projecting and assuming that my assistant was a woman. This is unconscious bias at play.

Find Your Fierce Exercise: For the next forty-eight hours, tune into your preferences and, if possible, your biases. Write down anything that shows up for you. If you go through the bank drive-through and the teller doesn't speak English as a first language, what is your reaction? When you see a heterosexual couple walking down the street where the woman is taller than the man, what is your reaction? If you see two people of the same gender walking arm in arm, what is your reaction? If you notice an email pop up in your inbox with a long name that you can't pronounce easily, what is your reaction? These are just examples to get you started. You may think you don't have bias with the examples I've provided, and perhaps that is true. Jot down those areas where preferences showed up for you and see if any could be an actual unconscious bias. Don't forget, these don't automatically make you a bad person. It's simply important to tune in and bring them to your consciousness so you can decide if there is anything you need to do about them.

HOLDING UP THE MIRROR

There are simple, quick things that organizations can do to interrupt imposter syndrome and ensure they are not promoting a culture that feeds it long term. The first step is being open to hearing feedback about the culture. So often people are holding up the mirror for us, if only we would listen. As an organization, you should review your promotion rates, evaluate and ensure pay equity, and seek feedback from those who are not in the majority. Be targeted with seeking that feedback, and be prepared to do something about what you hear. When you have a critical position to fill, ensure you are demanding a diverse slate of people be evaluated for the role, especially if it is for a senior position. Don't slot only the people you are comfortable with into positions. If and when you do decide to slot someone into a role, make sure it's the very best person for the job, and be transparent about why you took that approach. It's not that you can't make those decisions, but it is important to be transparent about your actions. This builds trust and helps people see where they stand.

Another way to successfully remove blind spots is to have what I call an "inclusion role" at the table. It's critical to have diverse people at the table, but if you're not there yet as an organization, assign someone to play the role of the inclusion advocate. Their job is to listen and speak from a place of the minority. They should ask questions from that position. Not only does it get voices heard that may not be currently sitting around the table, but it also creates empathy when you must walk in the shoes of someone else.

If you start to notice talented people pull back or begin to exhibit behaviors that look like imposter syndrome, as leaders you must lean in and get curious. Seek to understand what's going on to ensure a safe space for people to discuss.

Imposter syndrome is a complex issue. It doesn't stem only from corporate cultures. There are many places it can come from for someone. As a result, the solutions to combat it are not cut and dried, and they can also be quite complex. The first step for leaders and organizations that want their people to experience psychological safety and bring their best, fiercest self to the room is to take a stand for identifying areas that might need a bit of work.

> **Find Your Fierce Exercise:** If you are a leader in your organization, reflect on what you are doing that could be contributing to an environment that is ultimately feeding imposter syndrome for women and minorities. What systems or rules exist in your workplace that may not support people when they need that boost the most? Are you happy with your mix of women and minorities in leadership positions? While it can take a while to shift a culture, what microinequities or biases exist that you can do something about right now?

Whether you are reading this book from the standpoint of a person finding their personal fierce or an organization that wants to change and become more inclusive and stop fueling imposter syndrome for your team members, please don't go out and try all of these things at once.

You didn't arrive here in one day, so you won't change things in one day. In fact, trying to do that might instead confuse everyone around you, including yourself. Some of these tips and tricks won't resonate with you. That's OK. Remember the feedback coat scenario from chapter 8? Some of these solutions won't fit for you. Pick one or two and try them. Focus on it for a week or so, particularly when imposter syndrome rears its head and starts to wreak havoc. The goal with these interrupt tactics is not a complete overhaul of your life. It's a short-circuit in the moment to avoid going down a dark rabbit hole that doesn't serve you. Save the big stuff for the next section on Momentum.

Speaking of momentum, ready to build some? Here we go!

PART THREE

MOMENTUM

noun

mo·men·tum | \ mō-ˈmen-təm

Definition of *momentum**

strength or force gained by motion or by a series of
events

*from Merriam-Webster Dictionary

11

MOMENTUM TAKES MUSCLE

Momentum is a term from Newtonian mechanics within the field of physics, which is defined by Merriam-Webster as "strength or force gained by motion or a series of events." While I'm not intending to make you fierce physicists, the field does offer some salient examples for our topics in this book. As we have already discussed, individuals and corporations are complex systems. Other examples of complex systems can be seen all around us in nature. Theoretical physicist Per Bak referred to these systems as self-organized criticality (SOC), a type of organized instability that he wrote about in his book, *How Nature Works*:

> Complex behavior in nature reflects the tendency of large systems to evolve into a poised "critical" state, way out of balance, where minor disturbances may lead to events, called avalanches, of all sizes.

LIKE SAND THROUGH THE HOURGLASS . . .

A way to understand the concept of SOC is by visualizing a pile of sand. As sand continues to drop onto the pile, grain by grain, each individual grain is exerting force onto other grains and the pile as a whole. The sand pile becomes increasingly complex as the pile grows, with each additional grain of sand having the potential to cause an avalanche or perhaps to do nothing at all but organize itself, always on the critical edge—self-organized criticality.

No, there is no need to watch for avalanches at work unless you are a ski instructor. But sand piles in this case help to illustrate how in many circumstances things that look stable can in fact be remarkably unpredictable. In many cases, the relationship between input (grains of sand or changing personal habits) and output (avalanches or how we are perceived at work) can be shrouded in mystery. Another, perhaps more relevant concept from this example is that as more complexity is added to a system, it can become that much harder for an individual to effect change on the "pile" as a whole.

When Bak's theories were tested in a lab, the researchers found that after organizing itself into a small cone, the pile of sand would reach a critical state where one additional grain would cause an avalanche . . . or it would not. Researchers found that what was happening internally, inside the pile, as the grains shifted and adjusted to their surroundings became just as important as what happened to the pile as a whole. This is where

Bak's self-organized criticality and piles of sand come together with the frAIMwork: what happens to you in the work environment (what is happening to the pile) is as important as how you internalize it (what happens within the pile).

Every grain of sand in the pile has an effect on every other grain and is linked by unseen networks of pressure and tension. This final section of the book focuses on some of the deep work that is needed to affect change within these webs. These changes take deliberate intention and effort. It takes muscle to move the sand pile, to build the momentum necessary to create the change we want to see.

BLAZING A NEW (NEURAL) TRAIL

It takes repetition, routines, and rigor to have a sustainable result. The previous steps in the frAIMwork focused on Awareness and Interruption. These are valuable steps in the process, but in a way, they are a little like a Band-Aid. They stop the bleeding. They affect the symptoms. But in order to fully move out from under the weight of imposter syndrome, we need to spend time creating new habits and new thoughts around those habits. The reason this takes time is because as mentioned earlier, it takes time for a habit to fully take root. It takes time and repetition for new neural pathways to be developed.

The development of new neural pathways—taking full advantage of our complex, plastic brains—is an integral part of the deep work needed to change the sand pile. An example of this type of path blazing can be found in the treatment of obsessive compulsive disorder (OCD), a disorder characterized by recurring thoughts and ideas that can drive an individual to pursue repetitive behavior. A common treatment for OCD was (and still is) exposure therapy. The idea would be to expose a patient to their doubts, worries, or fears for gradually increasing periods of time. Additionally, cognitive therapy where the focus is on inaccurate or exaggerated thoughts is also used to treat OCD.

While both methods have had some success, psychologist Jeffrey M. Schwartz pioneered a new way to think about and treat OCD that may have applications for imposter syndrome as well. In Schwartz's research, he compared scans of the brains of those suffering from OCD and discovered functional differences between OCD patients and those without the disorder. The scans revealed how "mistakes" are exhibited in the human brain. In Norman Doidge's book, *The Brain That Changes Itself*, Schwartz explained mistakes as a three-step process. First, we get a "mistake feeling," which is a nagging sense that something is wrong. Second, we become anxious, and that anxiety drives us to correct the mistake. Third, when we have corrected the mistake, an automatic gear shift in our brain allows us to move on to the next thought or activity. Then both the mistake feeling and the anxiety disappear.

Unfortunately, the brain of an individual with OCD does not get to the automatic gear shift stage; it stays locked in place. This causes them to suffer from the nagging sense that something is wrong and anxiety-induced compulsions. These mistake false alarms are caused by the neural pathways and the signals traveling between different parts of the brain.

Schwartz's next step was to develop a treatment for OCD using his newfound knowledge. As Doidge put it in *The Brain That Changes Itself*:

> Schwartz wondered whether patients could shift the caudate manually by paying constant effortful attention and actively focusing on something besides the worry such as a new, pleasurable activity. This approach makes plastic sense because it "grows" a new brain circuit that gives pleasure and triggers dopamine release, which as we have seen rewards the new activity and consolidates and grows new neuronal connections.

Doidge went on to explain that Schwartz created a technique where he could help his patients separate themselves from the anxiety, and thus the compulsions, by helping them to focus on the fact that what an individual is experiencing is not in reality an attack of germs or leaving the stove on. Instead, they are experiencing their OCD. This important distinction allows a patient to create some distance from the content of the obsession and to simply (as with mindfulness, which we will cover below) observe their obsession's effect on them.

Once the focus has shifted to OCD itself and not the obsession, the next step is to refocus attention on a positive activity. As Doidge wrote, "With this treatment we don't so much break bad habits as replace bad behaviors with better ones." Each time that an obsession is sated, it creates a deeper and more ingrained neural pathway in the brain. As patients continue with the deep work of refocusing their attention onto a pleasurable activity, which in a sense is rearranging the grains of sand in their pile, they are actively blazing new paths in their brain. The practice does not offer immediate relief; however, it sets up lasting neuroplastic change. This change comes from repetition and routine by the OCD patient, and every imposter among us can benefit from the same type of rigor.

Schwartz's patients suffering from OCD were able to recognize the true source of their feelings and impulses, allowing them to focus on what they could do for long-term, successful treatment. Similarly, throughout this book we have explored how to become aware of our imposter feelings and then how to interrupt both our mind and our body. Throughout this momentum section of the book, we will examine opportunities to resolve these feelings of being an imposter, for the long term. This long-term resolution is made possible, at least in part, due to the plasticity of our neural pathways. To paraphrase Schwartz, the creation of new neural pathways will allow you to replace feelings of fraud with more accurate assessments of your accomplishments, goals, and abilities. This replacement, to end where we began in the world of physics and Per Bak, builds momentum as you complete the work inside your sand pile—one small change leads to another and another. These changes lead to a durable fierceness and long-term success no matter what the outside world may set against the outside of your sand pile.

Find Your Fierce Exercise: 10,000 steps a day. This is the goal that is preset on most fitness apps and fitbits. For some that is an achievable goal without much effort, but for others that may be too much. I challenge you to start walking. I don't care if it's 2,500 steps a day, please start. Think of it like piles of sand. You are only organizing to make it to the end of the day. Slowly, you will work up from there: 5,000 steps, 7,500 steps, soon 10,000 steps. Like an avalanche of sand, your steps will propel you to something greater. I promise you, each step will have an effect on the other steps, and who knows? One day you might be at 20,000 steps or more. Lace up those shoes and go do something good for yourself! What other piles of sand do you want to move for yourself? Go!

12

CHANGE YOUR BRAIN

Talking about sand piles and plastic brains is nice in theory, but what does this look like in the real world? What steps can be taken to actually create real change? This next chapter discusses methods and practices to implement changes in your brain. Just as discussed in previous chapters, your thoughts feed your actions, which, in turn, lead to your results. In many situations, the opposite is also true, with your actions altering your thoughts. From smiling to enhance your mood to slowing your breathing to calm anxious moments, there are a multitude of ways that the mind and body are connected. This chapter explores these connections and offers stories and examples meant to lead you toward positive change, which is a foundational element of building momentum in the frAIMwork.

PRACTICE SEEING HUMANS AS HUMAN

In chapter 3, Kelly talked about the signals she was sent from her family and how she had to call the school to verify for herself that she'd earned her degree. Throughout the interview, we discussed the situations that make her feel like an imposter the most. She described what happens to a lot of women in corporate America. "I feel extremely empowered when I'm around successful women who have reached whatever their definition of success is in their career and family life. When I'm around other successful women, it feels like we get each other," she said.

"It sucks to say it, but I feel smaller around men," she went on to say. "I feel like some men will make comments that will almost diminish my knowledge or my ability with a word or a side comment, and then I feel small and I feel like maybe I don't know what I'm talking about. I think, *Maybe I shouldn't be in this position.* That self-doubt kept me hiding in a large enterprise for a long time."

One way to practice working with people who intimidate you is to get curious and find out more about their lives. Even the people who look the most put together have struggled in some way. I've worked with hundreds of women, and I've never once come across anyone who didn't struggle in some way. When we can practice seeing other people as human and get curious enough to find out their stories—no matter how big their role, how large their paycheck, or how much further up the ladder they are—it can diffuse imposter feelings within moments.

It's important to remind yourself that we are all human and doing the best we can. More times than not, when I'm paired up with someone I think I won't have much in common with, I am surprised by how similar we are. It usually turns out that we want the same things or struggle with the same challenges. If you're open to that possibility, you can give each other really good strategies to take back and try.

The topic of parenthood came up many times in my interviews for this book. One theme I noticed among the parents is that they were all doing the best they could. It was like a safe space to confess that nugget of candor. Their voices would lower as though they were telling me a deep, dark secret that should never be spoken of again. Many shared that they always wanted to have kids, and most had fantastic role models for parents. Yet nothing would ever equip them for the questions they would face as parents themselves. One even said, "While there are a million books out there aimed to prepare you for parenthood, none of them actually can do the job fully. You just have to jump in with both feet and make it up!" I think that's a pretty healthy perspective on parenting, and I see a lot of similarities to the workplace. We are all trying to do the best we can.

Find Your Fierce Exercise: The next time you're with someone who triggers your feelings of imposter syndrome, flip what you're focusing on. Instead of assuming the person knows more than you or lamenting that the person's successes are making you feel small, get curious about the person. Ask about their background and seek to understand what their knowledge base actually is. It's OK for people to know different things and bring different talents to the table. Someone else having knowledge doesn't make you inferior. By shifting this perspective, you can figure out how your talents and strengths compliment theirs. Ask what one thing they wish they could do or know. Perhaps it just happens to be something you are really good at!

MINDFULNESS

Take a moment to think about your hands. They are holding this book, or tablet, or phone—however you are reading right now. Assuming it's a printed book, how does the paper feel between your fingers? Pay attention to the texture. Now smell the pages. Does it smell like an old library? Perhaps it smells a bit "woody." Keeping track of what page you're on, close the book and listen. Are you inside? Do you hear the soft whirring of a fan? Maybe you're outside, sitting in the sun. Feel the sun's warmth, hear the birds, smell the neighbor's fresh-cut grass.

What you did there—the intentional direction of attention to your senses in the present moment—is practicing mindfulness. Mindfulness as a concept is not an app or a trick or even meditation, specifically. While it is currently particularly buzzworthy, mindfulness is a practice pulled from Buddhism. The purpose of mindfulness is to notice your thoughts, feelings, and sensations without passing judgment. Over the past forty-five years, there have been myriad studies on the topic of mindfulness, trying to pinpoint exactly what it does for us and how (or even if) it helps. Much of the research shows that mindfulness can lead to stress reduction and an increase in positive thinking.

Probably the most famous form of active mindfulness is the practice of meditation. However, one can be mindful without meditating. For example, if you are out for a walk, try to be there in that moment, on that walk. If you're eating—eat; if you're cleaning—clean. If you're talking to a friend—be present to that conversation. The whole point of a mindfulness practice is that you are seeing and feeling but not judging.

Modern mindfulness is being marketed as a way to do everything from losing weight to being happy. The Buddhist monks who originated the practice, however, were not looking to be thin and cheerful but instead to change their sense of self and their perception of reality.

Fortuitously, this is exactly what you are looking to do as well. You're looking to change your current habits, find your fierce, and increase the success in your life. It is very possible that as you continue to practice mindfulness, you will learn to more fully experience the present moment in a nonjudgmental way, with less focus on the past or future. As the practice becomes more second nature, you might even find it becomes a more natural Interruption strategy. In fact, mindfulness could also help to overcome current habits of negatively judging yourself or others. This end goal aligns with some of the original intent of those meditating monks from long ago—changing your sense of self.

Find Your Fierce Exercise: Mindfulness exercises are plentiful when you search the internet. In fact, a quick search returned upward of twenty-seven million hits. Some are complex, but one that works particularly well is a technique called box breathing, which is used by everyone from professional athletes to doctors to Navy SEALS. This mindfulness technique will have you breathing in and out for counts of four. To do this exercise, sit upright in a chair with your feet flat on the floor. Place your hands in your lap with your palms facing up. Slowly exhale through your mouth so that all the oxygen leaves your lungs. Pay attention to what you're doing, and make sure all the breath is out. Next, inhale through your nose, count to four very slowly in your head, and feel the air completely fill your lungs and move into your abdomen. Hold your breath for another slow count of four, then exhale again through your mouth until all air is out of your lungs for the same slow count of four. Tune in to the feeling of the air leaving your lungs. Now hold your breath again for four counts. Repeat this process for as long as you'd like until you feel centered, calm, and completely aware of your breathing.

ADOPT A GROWTH MINDSET

All the way back in chapter 1, you learned the difference between a fixed mindset and a growth mindset. The book started with that delineation because it's one of the single most critical things a person needs in order to keep developing. Because it's so important, let's do a quick refresher. A growth mindset is the belief that a person's talents can be improved over time. People who have a growth mindset tend to be more oriented toward development and self-improvement. They believe how good you are is not nearly as important as believing in how good you want to be. Alternatively, people with a fixed mindset—the opposite of growth mindset—want to demonstrate that they are already intelligent or talented. They don't want to show that they don't have it all figured out yet or have weak spots or areas for development. Imposter syndrome is amplified when you operate from a fixed-mindset state.

People with a growth mindset also demonstrate tenacity and persistence when faced with challenges, because they see them as opportunities to learn and grow versus failures or signs of personal inadequacy. Carol Dweck, the pioneering authority on growth mindset and author of *Mindset: The New Psychology of Success*, believes it is one of the most critical components to career success.

Becky is someone I met through work and have known for over ten years now. Although work is what brought us together, we have remained friends long after our careers took us in different directions. There are so many life lessons we've shared with each other, we will probably always have a connection in one way, shape, or form. She agreed to be interviewed for this book and was asked to share some of her connections to imposter syndrome. This included how it's shown up for her and what she has done about it. Amazing wisdom came out through that conversation.

Throughout her life, there were times Becky pretended to be something. For example, when she took on a new role outside of the field she had been in for ten years, she felt the need to do a lot of the whole fake-it-til-you-make-it thing. "Even though I had a ton of transferable skills for the role, I felt this intense need to prove that I deserved to be there," Becky said. "And since I was doing that, I figured people must not really know me, and therefore my conclusion was that I didn't belong there. I didn't deserve to be at the table." As she reflected on it, she said the thing she's come to appreciate the most is that she wasn't alone—everyone is actually just making it all up. She talked about being a first-time parent and how nobody really knows how to be a good parent until this little person arrives and you have to figure it out. It's not something you've ever done before! "I think that is when I realized that it's true at work too," she said. "People are figuring out how to solve new challenges in business every single day, and they don't have all the answers either. I've come to appreciate that it's OK to be learning."

Becky is a lifelong ballet dancer. From the time she was a little girl she was in ballet and absolutely loved it. The discipline took a lot of time to develop, and as she became busier with her studies and other things in her life, she slowly pulled away from the activity in her adulthood. While it has been many years since she practiced ballet, Becky said her body falls right back into first position without much thought at all because it's such a comfort zone for her. A few years ago, she decided to find something good for her body to keep her active and continue to push herself to remain fit. The solution also needed to fit into her busy work schedule, so she signed up and went to her first early-morning CrossFit class. "I was bad at it," Becky said. "I mean really not strong at all, and all the moves were foreign to me. After the first class or two, I contemplated not going back. I kept running through all the things I wasn't good at and how it was so different from ballet. But then I realized I was looking at this as a glass-half-empty situation. I was focusing on all the things I wasn't good at, all the areas [where] I didn't have strength, instead of realizing that I had a lot of strengths to bring to the workout from the years of my ballet training. I had advantages over some of the strongest people in the gym because I have excellent balance and flexibility."

Becky realized that she needed to keep an open mind and a growth mindset if she was going to be successful with her CrossFit journey. This wasn't something she could fake until she made it. She challenged herself to focus on her strengths and started to notice that others in the class were learning from her as well. They realized that to be good at some of the exercises they needed balance and flexibility too, not only sheer strength. Had Becky continued to look at the situation through the lens of all her shortcomings when it comes to CrossFit, she probably wouldn't have gone back. She reflected on where she might be doing that in other parts of her life. "I quickly realized that if I don't leverage the strengths I do have and only focus on what's missing or how other people are doing something or defining success, I was not only missing opportunities to apply my unique talents but I would convince myself that I didn't belong, like I was a fraud, just faking it all," she said. "I was discounting what I did know!"

A growth mindset focuses on learning. It's not about the things you don't yet know, it's about the journey to learn them and continue to evolve as a human being. A fixed mindset is like stunting your growth. Not only does it fuel imposter syndrome, it keeps your true, authentic self bottled up. Many women interviewed for this book said they don't always pursue excellence out of fear of others finding out that they aren't perfect. Even though they intellectually know they don't have to be perfect, they set that expectation for themselves.

When asked where her growth mindset came from, Becky pointed to her strong support system, her clarity with her values, and knowing her boundaries, as well as being raised with a high level of psychological safety to try new things regardless of whether she was good or bad at them. "Those things have helped me to feel strong in who I am and not worry about whether I fit in or not," Becky said. "I'm not sure what I would do without that mindset. It's the key ingredient you need to be confident and good at being you!" Truer words have never been spoken, Becky. As the author of *Moving Past Perfect*, Thomas Greenspan, said, "Excellence is Risk. Perfectionism is Fear."

Find Your Fierce Exercise: Just as Becky reflected on how her unique skills and talents helped her and others in her CrossFit class, take some time to reflect on your unique gifts. What makes you uniquely you? Write down five things that you may have considered to be your imperfections or shortcomings in the past. Imagine a situation where those "imperfections" would be your secret superpower to balance things out and find a solution. Now, to directly apply this to your work life, write down a challenge you've faced recently where you felt you didn't have the right skill set or abilities to solve the problem. How could you reframe and leverage your "imperfections" to solve the problem? What additional steps could be taken to grow into any missing skills you haven't acquired yet?

UNCOVER YOUR BLIND SPOTS

Throughout this book, we've discussed how uncovering your blind spots is essential to growth and self-acceptance. It is also a key to building momentum toward finding your fierce and fighting imposter syndrome. As you'll recall, the first part of the frAIMwork is Awareness, and until you uncover your blind spots, awareness is hard to achieve. The thing about blind spots, though, is that we can't see them for ourselves until a story, experience, or interaction highlights them for us. You are blind to them. But once you know something, you can't unknow it. And once you know it, you get to choose whether you want to do something about it.

When you drive out of an alley where the hedges are overgrown on the corner and you try to cross the street, you might crash right into another car due to the blind spot. It shocks and disorients you. My friend recently told me a story that felt like the equivalent of trying to cross the street when I couldn't see. It totally shocked me but helped me to see one of my own unconscious biases and blind spots. The story is from a game in which the players ask yes or no questions to solve a mystery. See if you can figure out the riddle before you read the answer at the end.

A father and son are in a horrible car crash that sadly kills the father. The son is rushed to the hospital and requires emergency surgery. As he is about to go under the knife, the surgeon looks at his face and exclaims, "I can't operate on this boy!" When others in the operating room ask why not, the surgeon says, "Because the boy is my son." How is this possible?

I spent a few minutes on this question when my friend posed it to me. My first reaction was that it was a trick question. I guessed that the wording of the story said a father and son were in an accident, but it didn't say they were father and son to each other. Wrong answer. Then I thought, "Of course! The accident victim was gay and his partner was the surgeon, and that was actually his son too." Possible, but wrong again. One last theory I came up with was that the "father" who died in the crash was a chaplain, perhaps on his way to church with a member of his congregation. And the boy's actual father was the doctor in the ER. Nope. After several rounds of yes/no questions and getting the answer incorrect, my friend revealed the answer: the surgeon was the boy's mother.

You could have knocked me over with a feather. I mean, I do this work every day. I fight the good fight around gender equity and awareness of where we are reinforcing bias. I talk about how women need to be heard and viewed equally. Yet I completely missed it.

That riddle stumped me because I was caught in my paradigm. Sure, it's a paradigm I've been handed through social norms, assumptions, and biases. But nonetheless, it blindsided me. My brain was wired to assume the surgeon was a man. I did a quick internet search and found most people assume the surgeon is a man. But now that I know it's a woman, I can't unknow it, and it changes the choices I can make. It has rewired my brain.

Find Your Fierce Exercise: What did you experience when you read the surgeon riddle? Did it uncover anything for you? Are there times in your life you can remember having a blind spot revealed? What were they? What happened and what were the circumstances? Reflect on how you can introduce more experiences or conversations into your life that help you uncover more of your assumptions and biases.

KNOW YOUR VALUES AND YOUR VALUE

There is a difference between values and value. When you know your values, you understand the set of principles or standards of behavior that are most important to you in your life. When you know your value, you know what you are worth. Let's explore this a bit further. We'll start with values.

KNOW YOUR VALUES

Do a Google search for discovering your core values and you will be inundated with executive and life coaches who are poised to help you uncover your personal values. Unless asked (or forced) to articulate what their values are, most people haven't really thought about it. They can typically tell if something has violated a value, but they may not be completely tuned in and aware of why it feels so bad. According to Barb Markway and Celia Ampel in *The Self-Confidence Workbook*, values are "the principles that give our lives meaning and allow us to persevere through adversity." That definition is one I like because it doesn't only give the textbook definition of what a value is, it also explains why they are so important. Our values are what get us through the hard parts of life.

Values come from a lot of places—our religion, our family, our ancestral culture, and the societies we live in. At an early age, our values are likely given to us. We are told what we should care about. As we grow, we discover which values are truly ours. These come from experiences, hardships, and tough decisions we need to make about what is most important to us. If asked right now, you could probably write down a decent list of words that you feel are your personal values, but that list might be shorter than the actual values you have. Unless you've done some deep personal value discovery, you may not be totally aware of all your values.

During my own personal values discovery journey, I went through a coaching certification program and was partnered with someone who was my peer coach. We were doing some deep work to identify and articulate our core personal values. One of the values I identified for myself was Choice. My peer coach and I discussed why this was such an important thing to me and therefore one of my values. "I don't want to have a scarcity mentality or limiting beliefs, so it's really important to me to have choices in my life. By having choice, it frees me from any limitations and keeps me on a journey of growth," I said. My peer coach listened but pressed me on whether this was truly one of my values. The role of a coach is to press your thinking and push you to explore and become self-aware, but I was getting a little irritated with him. I kept thinking, *These are my values and I think I would know better than you would.*

To help me see what he was seeing, he asked me what my two favorite vegetables were in the whole world. Easy: broccoli and carrots. He then asked me what my two most hated vegetables were in the whole world. Also easy: green peppers and celery. He said, "Great. Teresa, for lunch today would you like green peppers or celery?" Ick. Neither. I wanted the choice of broccoli and carrots instead. He said, "Those aren't an option. You want choice. You value choice. Here's your choice: green peppers or celery?"

Ahhhh, light bulb! My core personal value wasn't choice after all. What I really value is input and contribution to my choices, not simply having the choices themselves. For the longest time I was so sure my value was choice, when really it was having a voice to contribute to the choices I have for myself. Two very different things and an important distinction to have clarity with.

The more in tune with your values you are, the more confident you will feel standing up for yourself or speaking up. Keep in mind there are no right or wrong values, no problematic values. The only time values become problematic is when you are not clear on what yours are, as illustrated above. When feelings of imposter syndrome show up and the going gets tough, knowing the core values that you operate by and hold yourself accountable to will reassure you that you are working in alignment toward those values, even when you feel like a fraud or as if you don't belong. To be happy, successful, and authentic as you strive for your goals requires you to live by your values. And while realizing all the goals you set out for yourself may not be achievable, living by your values is something you have 100 percent control over once you know what they are.

Find Your Fierce Exercise: Knowing your values gives you confidence. But when you're asked what your values are, it can be hard to make that list. Let's do an exercise to help you with this. For this exercise, think about the people you consider to be your heroes and (s)heroes. They can be historical figures, family members, or people you've encountered throughout your life. List reasons why you have strong admiration toward these people and why you consider them your heroes. Be specific about what they do that inspires you. Doing this can help you understand the things that are most important to you. The behaviors of your heroes likely exemplify something you value. For example, one of my heroes is my husband because he is endlessly patient and supportive of my dreams. I've come to learn that supportiveness is one of my core values. If you have trouble articulating the things you value in your heroes, Dr. Russ Harris, author of the book *The Confidence Gap*, has generously made available to the public for free a list of fifty-plus common values that you can use as a reference.

Once you have a good list identified, try to narrow the list down to no more than seven values you resonate with most strongly as your personal core values. Next, identify what your top three core values are—your non-negotiables. If you were forced to only articulate three things you stand for and are most important to you, what are they? This will clarify for you your foundation and who you are as a person. The more aware you are of that, the stronger your confidence in being unapologetic about who you are. It's impossible to be a fraud when you are living in alignment with your top values.

KNOW YOUR **VALUE**

Knowing your personal values is different than knowing your value or market worth. You have unique skills and strengths that you bring to the party. Even skills that are prevalent in the workplace are different when delivered by you because of your unique take on them. The workplace today is full of talented, smart, ambitious people bringing innovation and big ideas to the table. It can be intimidating if you let it be. It can also make it difficult to know what your true market value is. To advocate for yourself and defend your worth, you must know the going rate for the contributions you provide to an organization. That starts with knowing your strengths and skills first, then understanding what the market is willing to pay for those things. If you don't know what your skills are worth in the marketplace and demand a fair wage for them, why would anyone else do that for you? When imposter syndrome is most active, it will have you believing that you are not good enough at what you do and that you don't have anything unique that couldn't be replaced in a heartbeat. While it's true we are all technically replaceable at work, there is unique value you give to your teams and workplaces, every day.

The first thing you must establish is the going rate for the services you are providing. Salaries can vary widely depending on the size and industry of the company. Not surprisingly, bigger organizations can pay more, and smaller organizations tend to have smaller budgets. However, smaller organizations may connect their employees more tightly to the mission and also be able to offer great accountability and exposure with senior leaders, which in the long run can provide great developmental experience for employees.

Even once you've determined the work you are doing and the going rate, you must also realistically evaluate your performance in the role compared to others doing similar work. This takes time and self-reflection to accomplish. However, once this work is done, online resources such as Salary.com and Glassdoor.com can be a useful starting point for helping you determine the average going rate, by location, for the services you are providing. I say starting point because you need to know that this information is self-reported, so it may not be an entirely accurate picture of what the market value is for a role. In addition to reading up on these sources, I recommend you lean in to your network to gain knowledge that is helpful in knowing the worth of the position you hold.

I also encourage people to do informational interviews. In the modern workplace, people are opting in every day. An organization can't require someone to stay. That said, there are so many things they can do to help an employee opt in as they hop in the car and drive to the office. The primary way that someone can feel good about the job they are going to in the morning is to know that they are valued and they make a fair wage. By doing informational interviews, you have the ability to understand if your skill set is in demand and appropriately valued. The time to know this information is not when you desperately need a new job, so do your homework and keep your finger on the pulse of what is a hot skill and valued.

In addition to paying off in a monetary sense, knowing your worth and ensuring you are paid for the skills that you bring to your work will further fight any fraud feelings that pop up. Knowing your value and worth is critical because it will set you up for success in the long run and is an integral part of the momentum stage of the frAIMwork.

Take writing this book as an example. I am not a psychologist. I have not conducted endless social experiments to test the statistical significance of imposter syndrome on rates of promotion in leadership positions within a corporation. As I was gathering information to include in this book, I had so many moments where I questioned if what I was offering would have value. What was my opinion worth? The thing is, my opinion is valuable because I have over twenty-five years of direct business experience where I have observed firsthand the impact that imposter syndrome has on people and organizations. Not to mention people in my extensive network who were willing to share their experiences and wisdom with you, and furthermore, my own personal experiences. You can see where I'm going with this. When you add that all up, I have way more than twenty-five years of expertise to share. That uniquely positions me to write this book, to share my experience, wisdom, information curation, and dot connecting. There is a unique value to that.

People have shared with me that knowing they have the tools and power to offer unique insights that have value is one of the single most game-changing pieces of information for their careers and lives. It's not only about placing a price tag on it but also about knowing that value is generated by their voice being heard—a value not just anyone could generate.

Find Your Fierce Exercise: Review your answers and reflections from some of the previous Find Your Fierce exercises, especially the ones that pertain to your strengths and unique viewpoints and contributions. Do you know what your skill set is worth in the open marketplace? In addition to resources like Salary.com or Glassdoor.com, who in your network can you tap into for valuable insights? For example, you may not be able to come out and ask a peer in your network, "Hey, how much do you make?" but you could ask something like, "How much would you expect a role like X to make at your company?" As you collect more data, you can see a trend and average emerge as to the going market value for your skills. Even more important than the dollar amount, you are the only person who has your unique view of the world and interpretation of facts. That is valuable. Make sure you are paying close attention, and don't ever give a discount on your fierce . . . for anyone.

ENTER THE FLOW STATE

Remember that in the growth-mindset section we talked about the importance of just getting started. Sometimes taking that first step is actually the biggest one. Just start. Once you are in the flow of something, it's easier to continue and even build greater momentum.

My sister-in-law Heidi is self-assured, smart, and confident. Not only is she a family member, she is someone I've always looked up to as a role model for fierceness, so I interviewed her for this book and asked her about her own experiences with imposter syndrome. She spent nearly thirty years as a school counselor helping kids navigate their feelings and challenges. A bit later in her career, she decided to become a licensed professional counselor so that she could treat individual, private clients. To gain that licensure, she had to take a big exam. "I thought, *There's no way I'm going to pass this. I haven't taken an exam in twenty-five years!*" she exclaimed. Not only did she pass, but she passed with an exceptionally high score. She was clearly qualified and ready. However, once she began counseling individuals, her imposter thoughts flared up again.

"When I started doing therapy with clients, I remember feeling like, *I can't believe they're letting me work with clients! What do I know?*" she said. "But, when I'm actually in a session and we're face-to-face, I know exactly what I'm doing, and I always feel competent. Truth be told, I have these moments like I'm going to be found out that I have my own issues. I'm not a perfect human being. I know that no one expects me to be, but it's a weird thing your brain does. I just have to get in front of my clients and I'm back to my confident self."

Heidi illustrated perfectly what happens when we enter what positive psychology researcher Mihaly Csikszentmihalyi calls the flow state. The flow state happens when we are fully engaged in what we're doing and let our ego and inner critic be silenced. This flow state completely holds our attention, so our minds don't have the bandwidth to both worry and do the activity at the same time. The next time you're feeling like an imposter with something you're working on, jump into the action of whatever it is. Write the proposal. Get on stage. Talk to that person. Do the work. That action will engage your mind and reduce the likelihood that you'll let imposter thoughts run away with you.

I recently listened to Amy Poehler's book *Yes, Please!* In her preface, she also talks about how hard it is to write a book. (Amy—call me, we need to talk. I feel you!) She says you simply need to do it. It's not the worrying about whatever you're worrying about that's important. It's the doing. She says, "put your brain in a drawer," get productive, and start. It's not in the act of stressing about the activity or wondering if you are good enough to do it. It's much more about the act of doing something and taking action. That's called getting in the flow. Act to determine what your next act is. One thing at a time. Putting one foot in front of the other is how you run marathons.

When you do this, you are literally building momentum, which is what this stage of the frAIMwork is all about.

Find Your Fierce Exercise: Are you aware of when you are in the flow state? Write down, in detail, the circumstances in which you find yourself in the flow state. This includes times when you are fully using your skills and talents, lose track of time because you are so engaged in the activity, or feel complete control over the situation. These are signs of being in the flow state. Being aware of when you are in your flow state allows you to harness your power and take back confidence that you do belong, and you are fierce.

13

CHANGE YOUR LIFE

Changing your brain and reframing challenges allows you to change your actions. This, in turn, will lead to changes in your life. By following the frAIMwork you've begun to build momentum, and this momentum will continue to build as you work through the pieces of this chapter. The steps outlined below will, at times, be difficult, but by incorporating them into your normal, daily activities, you will begin to see positive changes in your life.

GET COMFORTABLE BEING UNCOMFORTABLE

This is a difficult one. When you need to stand up and name things that are not OK, it is uncomfortable. As humans we seek comfort, and for the most part we don't try to put ourselves in situations that make us uncomfortable. This is where it's important to know what your values are and let people know when they bump up against your boundaries. It requires us to be honest with ourselves, our friends, and our organizations and tell the truth about the hard parts.

This can lead to uncomfortable conversations, and many women have been conditioned by society to be more accommodating than truth-telling. "Go along to get along" and "help make people feel comfortable" are messages many women have received throughout their lives.

I sometimes get angry that I have to do so much damn truth-telling all the time. That there is so much that still needs to change to have equal opportunities, and yet it's also my job to help change it. Large-scale culture shifts don't happen overnight, and they require us to be bold and demand a change. This is probably the hardest part about the Momentum section of the frAIMwork and the steps you will take to change your life. The reason it's hard is because it takes a long time and requires unapologetic resolve. You may have heard this saying: *What you permit you promote.* And it's true. If something isn't working for you and you don't speak up and say something about it, you're agreeing to it. We teach people how to treat us every day by either sticking up for ourselves or not. When someone treats you poorly and you don't say anything about it, you're basically saying you're okay with being treated that way.

Something else that has been permitted for too long is allowing others to label and define us as individuals. Labeling by others impacts people in significant ways, and in order to change this situation, it's important to speak up and say that labels aren't OK. Another point in *Yes, Please!*, Amy Poehler's book, that struck a chord for me was when she highlighted that women are constantly being asked to define themselves. These definitions could include labels such as "I'm the cynical one" or "I'm the heavy comedian, I tell fat jokes" and so on. The point isn't so much the actual label, it is that we—as women— are expected to fit into a specific box or category. This is extremely limiting for the individual who has been labeled, and also limiting for all women as it implies that there can only be one "heavy one" or only one "cynical one." Women are constantly being scrutinized, judged, and devalued by the use of these labels.

Not only have we been labeled, as Poehler points out, we are also still expected to compete against each other. In fact, the most insidious part of the labeling practice is that it frequently makes the competition among women for a limited number of roles in an organization that much more competitive. The grouping and classification that society submits women to leads them, in many cases, to mistrust the very people they should be trusting the most: other like-minded, similarly experienced women. We end up questioning their expertise and experience and then, subconsciously, questioning our own. Men, on the other hand, also compete for things, but we don't walk around asking them to define themselves. Why do women need a definition in order to stand out? We are enough.

Yet labeling and permitting poor treatment still happens day in and day out. It's hard to tell someone when they've violated a value. Especially if you feel you are expected to act a certain way and the stakes feel high if you step outside that box or definition. Until we tell the truth about the hard parts, people may not know they've crossed a boundary.

Find Your Fierce Exercise: If you're working within an organizational culture that's not set up to be as healthy as it could be—maybe it's overly competitive, or its structure or people do not create psychological safety for you—it's important to understand your own personal boundaries and say something if need be. This will take courage. Do you need to speak up? To whom? Can you help to shift the culture in some way? Do you need to leave and find a better work environment? What do you need in order to be your best and do your best? These questions can make us uncomfortable. The conversations that follow may also feel uncomfortable. But getting more comfortable with uncomfortable conversations is one of the most important things you can do to find your voice and tell the truth about the hard parts. Doing so will change your life.

BUILD YOUR PERSONAL
BOARD OF DIRECTORS

One of the invaluable things I learned from a mentor early in my career was to build my own personal board of directors. Several years back, my mentor challenged me to think of the different types of people I would want to support and guide me through my career. A company's board of directors is made up of people from different industries and areas of expertise. They are assembled to give an organization the broadest set of inputs to ensure success. Similarly, I needed to assemble a diverse group of people with varied experience and perspectives to provide me with advice and guidance throughout my career journey.

Sometimes I need a soft-spoken type who is always there for me, like a trusty blanket when I'm feeling bad. Sometimes I need a cheerleader type who will be upbeat and positive, no matter what I'm facing, always helping me see the bright side. And sometimes I need a tough-love type who delivers a swift kick in the pants to shake me out of my pity party. As I reflected on the different people in my network who could fill those different roles for me, I began to assemble my virtual personal board of directors.

Personal connection is one of the most powerful tools we have available to us as humans. It's critical that we leverage it. For example, one day I was at a casual networking event with another woman in my field. I'd relied on her many times for a reality check because she always tells it like it is. I turned to her and said, "I kind of feel like I don't know what I'm doing sometimes. It's like I feel like I just stumbled through life and ended up here. Ever feel that way?" She too had been in the field a long time, and I expected her to say I was crazy. Instead, she said, "Honey, we all feel that way. It's not just you. Get out of your head." Knowing I wasn't the only one who feels that way from time to time helped so much. And her matter-of-fact delivery made me laugh and get out of my own way!

If you're facing an intimidating career challenge or moment and are feeling like you don't know what you're doing, reach out to the person on that board who will serve you the most at that time. The time to build your network is not when you need it. It's like credits in a bank. You need to deposit them and invest the time and energy into the relationship so that when the time comes to make a withdrawal, the resources are there for you. The time to build your personal board of directors is now.

Find Your Fierce Exercise: Take out a sheet of paper. Draw a circle in the middle of it. Think of this like a big, round boardroom table. Next, draw several smaller circles around the big circle. Make sure you put at least four to six circles on the page. These smaller circles represent the chairs that your personal board of directors will sit in. In each of the circles, write the different types of roles you want your board members to play. This can be things like "cheerleader" or "boss lady" or "hugger." Reflect on those people in your network you can rely on to always fill those roles when you need them to. Write their names in the circles. Share with that person exactly why you put them on your board of directors and the value you get from them. This is a form of contracting with them, and they'll know the best way to support you when you need it. An added benefit is that it also makes them feel good that they are helpful to you! The next time you're feeling out of your depth, reach out to someone you feel comfortable sharing your feelings with and talk about your fears and anxieties. Most times, you'll find that other people have had the same feelings in one part of their life or another. You're not alone in this.

JOURNAL EVERY DAY

As humans, we are all made up of stories. Most are stories we were told growing up, and some are stories we tell ourselves. It might be the recounting of an event or our memory of something. The crazy thing is that sometimes those stories are accurate, and many, many times they are skewed. Few of us can recount the exact specifics from our childhood, but they are operating beneath our subconscious. Those details of the story influence our thoughts and actions. They infiltrate what we believe about ourselves and what we tell others outwardly or subtly through our actions. In short, our stories become our identity. Yet we rarely examine our personal stories for actual truth. We just believe them.

The journey to having an accurate reflection of yourself requires you to hit pause on those autopilot thoughts and reactions to situations. By doing this we can uncover and learn the real stories about who we are. That's super important because that is who we want running the show. This also allows us to reprogram our unconscious thoughts to tap into the neuroplasticity of our brains.

There is a reason you've been given assignments focused on reflection and journaling throughout this book. Journaling has been proven to help people prioritize thoughts and manage stress. It also provides an opportunity to recognize things that have a triggering effect for you. Most important, journaling allows you space for positive reinforcement, encouragement, and self-talk.

Find Your Fierce Exercise: By this point in the book, I've asked you to journal . . . a lot. Take a moment to consider the importance of journaling. What have you learned so far by journaling your answers to the previous Find Your Fierce exercises? How has journaling helped you to find your fierce and manage your feelings of imposter syndrome? Prior to this book, had you journaled? If so, why? How helpful was it then? Lastly, how could journaling continue to benefit you as you make changes to overcome imposter syndrome and own your success, creating the life and career you've always wanted?

CULTIVATE COURAGE

When you are feeling most fearful, do not retreat. Remember back to chapter 2, when we discussed personal beliefs and expectations, that there are four responses to a threat: fight, flight, freeze, or fawn. Flight, which means to run away from the problem or threat, is a common response to fear. In the case of imposter syndrome, when it makes you fearful about being found out or discovered to be not as great as someone thought you were, flight is one of the worst responses. Please don't retreat. These feelings of self-doubt are being triggered by things your brain is tricking you into believing. Now is not the time to run away. Now is the time for that Wonder Woman pose.

In a recent international study led by Adam Radomsky, PhD, professor of psychology at Concordia University and editor-in-chief of the *Journal of Behavior Therapy and Experimental Psychiatry,* researchers discovered that 93.6 percent of the people studied in nonclinical populations at fifteen sites in thirteen countries across six continents reported experiencing at least one intrusive thought during the past three months. The study found that the most reported category of intrusive thoughts was self-doubt.

Let that one sink in for a minute. That's basically *all* of the people surveyed on six continents struggling with feelings of self-doubt. This fear caused by self-doubt is very much a human experience. Guess what happens when I've asked workshop participants to raise their hand if they've ever felt one of the following: Fear of looking like an idiot. Fear of being found out. Fear of letting people down. Fear of getting it wrong. Fear of being too much. Fear of not being enough. Fear of sounding different. Fear of looking different. Fear of being different. Fear of failure. Fear of success. Fear of rejection. Fear of being hurt. Fear of not belonging. Everyone in the audience raises their hand, because fear is part of our human condition.

Dr. Brené Brown, a research professor, TED Talk expert, and one of my own personal heroes, who has studied vulnerability, worthiness, shame, and courage extensively, says, "People buy into [fear] and feel fear because they don't have the language to attach to what it is. We're all afraid. We just have to get to the point where we understand it doesn't mean that we can't also be brave."

We all feel moments of self-doubt and have struggled with fear. Instead of isolating ourselves when we feel this way, it is more helpful to realize it's a human response. We are humans. To gain momentum, you need to cultivate courage and calm the imposter feelings. Remember your board of directors? Get those folks on speed dial, because you may need to make a few phone calls when you're feeling vulnerable.

Find Your Fierce Exercise: What are some of your fears regarding your career? How about fears you have about your relationships? Get out your list of your personal board of directors . . . now is the time to leverage them. Discuss with a trusted member of your board one of the fears you are feeling. Ask for another perspective on the fear. As the saying goes, "When you share a fear or burden with someone it is cut in half; when you share a joy or triumph with someone it is doubled." Tuck the sharing of a joy or triumph away for another day and commit to doing it, but for now, share that fear. It will cut that fear in half, help you gain a new perspective, and allow you to move forward in a productive way.

DANCE TO YOUR OWN SONG

You met Emily earlier in the book back in chapters 2 and 5, where she shared her experiences with imposter syndrome. She had recently been contemplating a job change within her organization. She noticed a need for a coaching program within the suite of offerings her company provided to clients, and she created a strong business case for why it was so critical. The company liked it and asked her if she wanted to take over the program, but she'd have to step down from her COO role to do it. At first she turned it down. "It's like you're trying to scale that wall and get up on the roof, to prove you can be on the roof, even though you don't want to be on the roof," she said. "You don't think about what's going to happen when you get up there. When I made it to the roof, I thought, *Oh my god, I am mapping my career to someone else's definition of success.* If I was being honest with myself, what I really wanted was to lead that coaching practice."

Emily reported that the company was not going to change her compensation, but she would need to leave the COO job to take the coaching role. She worried that other people would think she'd failed at the COO role. Eventually, Emily decided to leave the COO position and take the role she really wanted. Now she's creating her own vision of what success means to her. Emily shared that the whole experience has been quite freeing. When she stopped worrying about what others thought and followed the beat of her own drum and started dancing to her own song, she was immediately freed up from thinking she wasn't enough or didn't fit in.

In corporate America, we put all kinds of currency and value into the titles we hold. People wonder what's wrong with you if you don't want the path that most people define as success. And these perceptions result in real repercussions, including someone feeling pressure to follow a certain path or excel in areas that aren't their true passion. This doesn't create a safe space to explore our gifts and feel valued for what we bring. The suggestion here is not necessarily to leave your job like Emily did, but her story can help us all assess our own paths. Are you going after something because it's what you're "supposed" to do to succeed or because it's your own vision of what you want to do to be successful? When you become clear about the song you want to be dancing to, it's difficult to feel like you don't belong on the dance floor.

Find Your Fierce Exercise: Take a moment to define what success means to you. What does it look like and feel like? What are you doing each day? Does your dream job have a title (e.g., vice president, teacher, doctor) or is it more of a description of the outcomes you produce (e.g., selling things, helping people, saving lives)? This is a good opportunity to draw from the personal core values work you did previously. List as many types of jobs as you can think of that involve either doing those things you wrote down or outcomes you want to achieve. As you do this, don't judge the title. For example, collecting garbage is a way of helping people and providing a tremendous service, but if titles are important, you might feel inclined to dismiss that career path if you judge it as "garbage person." Now that you have this list, jot down some concrete steps you can take to make this dream a reality. Maybe it involves a big move like changing careers, but perhaps it means a smaller change like volunteering more in areas you are passionate about.

FIND YOUR CREW AND HAVE EACH OTHER'S BACK

Having a strong network of people who have your back and whose backs you have will create psychological safety and help you combat feeling like a fraud. When you have a group of people you know will come to your defense or support you when you need it most, you are more likely to speak up and be brave. This doesn't need to be an exclusive exercise. The point is not to band together with only women or only men or only people of color. Diversity is a great value to adhere to and strive for. It takes all different types of perspectives and teammates to reach the best solution. What is important is to find people you trust and can empathize with your situation and help you to be successful.

Have you ever shared an idea in a meeting only to be met with a lukewarm reaction or blank stares? Then shortly after, someone else says essentially the exact same thing and everyone practically applauds? It happens a lot, particularly to women and minorities. Recently this experience was given a name when astronomer Nicole Gugliucci tweeted, "My friends coined a word: 'hepeated.' For when a woman suggests an idea and it's ignored, but then a guy says the same thing and everyone loves it." The tweet was picked up and shared thousands of times over, with women responding that this happens to them on a daily basis. In addition, it was pointed out that this happens to Black and ethnic minorities as well. This phenomenon occurs more times than I'd care to admit, particularly in the workplace. Jessica Bennett, author of *Feminist Fight Club*, took this concept one step further, saying that culprits of hepeating are called himitators. While this may be a humorous way to name what's happening, it still happens, so what's a girl to do?

In 2016, the *Washington Post* wrote an article about a

group of women in the White House who banded together and started to use the technique of amplification to ensure each other's ideas were heard when hepeating and himitating started to happen to them. Female White House staffers and aides used a rhetorical technique to stop interruptions or prevent others from stealing ideas as their own (on purpose or otherwise) by reinforcing the points made by other women around the table. When someone, particularly another woman, made a good point, another woman would repeat and reinforce that the credit should go to the original woman offering the idea. It was recounted that it made the idea much harder to ignore or steal, and that even President Obama himself started to notice and call on more women more frequently in meetings.

In chapter 4 we discussed the importance of sharing language others have used to describe you as a means of getting comfortable tooting your own horn. The concept of amplification and having someone in your crew who brags for you is an even more deliberate action. Bennett further references the importance of finding a "hype man," which is someone who boasts for you and whom you boast for in return. Your crew can do it for you, and you can do it for your crew. Research shows it works!

Find Your Fierce Exercise: Take inventory of your close colleagues and coworkers. Who can you amplify, and who can you ask to help amplify you? How can you amplify an idea? When you notice someone else taking credit for an idea, try saying something like, "I'm glad you agree with Sarah's idea. As she said . . ." then repeat and amplify the idea, giving credit back to Sarah. It takes a village, always remember that. Find your crew.

14

ORGANIZATIONS NEED CHANGING TOO

In the words of the great Eleanor Roosevelt, "No one can make you feel inferior without your consent." While that is true, and we've spent a lot of time together throughout this book exploring what you can do as an individual to change your brain and take different actions that will change your life to fight imposter syndrome, this is not the only part of the solution. The systems we are a part of shape how we feel. As we discussed in chapter 5, corporate culture can be one of the many contributing sources of fuel for imposter feelings.

Like a pebble in a pond creating ripples and impacting the entire body of water, all individuals can be powerful agents of change. There is power within each of us to create the change we would like to see in our respective organizations. This fact should not be glossed over. You are all empowered in some way to resolve the issues you face every day.

However, in our current corporate structure, the vast majority of change and cultural norms come from the leadership level within an organization or a business. So if you are reading this book and you are at this level, you have even more influence to change the system. As you read the previous chapters, you might have seen yourself in some of the examples. Perhaps you have even experienced impostor syndrome yourself. But now you are at a level in your company that imbues you with special power, and, just like in *Spider-Man*, "with great power comes great responsibility."

With the majority of change in your business coming from your level, you have a unique ability to change your organization. You can work to make the environment more open to diverse ways of thought and more accepting of different backgrounds, and you can help eliminate the factors that allow imposter syndrome to thrive in your organization. But you have to take notice of those situations when they occur and evolve the fibers of the organization. The system needs to change in order to reap the benefits of diversity and prevent people who are different from feeling like a fraud.

In this chapter, the stories will tee up common situations that occur in organizational settings so that we can unpack them and explore the importance of recognizing them and changing responses and actions. The organizational culture will become one that supports different people, makes them feel like they belong, and helps them to find their fierce. If you are a leader in your organization, this chapter is particularly for you, so take it to heart.

ACTIONS SPEAK LOUDER THAN WORDS—MAKE YOURS COUNT

Many organizations say the right things. They want diversity. They want people to feel valued. They want to create a safe space for their employees to thrive and grow. But it's not enough to say these things. What is said versus the actions taken is often where the disconnect happens.

In chapter 5, we discussed the research from the World Economic Forum regarding the different reactions to whether significant progress had been made to advance women in the workplace. Men and women surveyed had vastly different perspectives on that answer. Now is the time for organizations to align on this and reflect on what they are doing to either promote or squelch disparities across genders. Top-down commitment is critical to building the leadership pipeline and quieting environments that feed imposter syndrome. If you want equity, you have to act in an equitable way.

Being in HR, I get asked to meet with a lot of people to assess fit for a role. For example, I can't tell you the number of times throughout my career that I've been asked by a senior leader to meet with a friend's kid who recently graduated from college and see where we might find a spot for them in the organization. I'm always happy to help people get connected and have the opportunity to shine, but a stark difference I've noticed in these conversations is the orientation and mindset that the people come to the table with. The following story illustrates how that difference shows up most notably between how men and women approach the conversation, and what leaders need to do to keep the playing field level.

Hank had recently graduated with a degree in sociology, and his father knew one of the executives I was working with. I was asked to meet with Hank, learn about his interests, and help him navigate the organization to find a possible role he could apply for. Hank spent his last semester of college at sea on a cruise ship learning hands-on leadership. In our conversation he said that he knew he would need to start out at the bottom of the company and work his way up, but he knew he could do it. I thought to myself it was great that he was acknowledging that although his father was well connected, he would still need to put in the work. However, the conversation quickly turned to the things he did and did not want to do. "I like big-picture things, don't like to spend much time in the weeds, and while I know how to use Excel, I don't want to do that for very long," Hank said. "I find it boring. I was looking at some of the jobs on your website, and I think I'd like to be a regional account leader. I think within a relatively short amount of time with the company, I should be ready to do that. Maybe six to twelve months? I'm an extremely fast learner."

Hank was confident but lacking self-awareness of how

ready he was to do the job, as it required five to seven years of applicable experience, plus one to three years leading others and experience selling and pitching ideas and products. I suggested we spend some time discussing the different roles that might *prepare* him for a role like that down the road. Perhaps project coordination, data analysis, or supporting the development of a product. He was adamant that his semester at sea had taught him most of what he likely needed to know and that he would learn quickly as he went. He shared that he'd led a team to get PADI certified and take their first dive. He'd also had to pitch his idea for a process that would get people in the water quicker, which would improve the other students' satisfaction with the training. Hank's story perfectly illustrates the types of conversations I regularly have with men. They ask for things beyond their reach and assume they will learn fast and ultimately be successful.

In contrast, several weeks after my meeting with Hank, I was given the resume of a young woman named Betty who was internal to the company. We met to discuss what she was interested in doing next. She had been there for three years and spent time in a product development role and a project manager role, and had started managing a small team about nine months earlier. Betty was interested in a regional account manager role she'd seen posted. However, she had not done any direct sales yet. She talked about how her knowledge of products would likely help her in the role but pointed out that technically she was three months shy of the requisite one to two years of team management. She spent quite some time acknowledging that she had not done direct sales and worried that could hinder her ability to land a role like this.

Given she was internal to the organization, I suggested she meet with the executive to discuss what she wanted to do and the type of role she was interested in. "I'd love to meet with him, but I don't meet all the requirements of the role yet," Betty said. "The last thing I want to do is waste his time if I'm not ready." After some urging, Betty agreed to meet with him. Betty's story illustrates the types of conversations I have with women. They focus on their gaps and are humble about their accomplishments, almost to a fault. While they might also believe they can be successful, they make sure they are not overselling their capabilities.

When I debriefed with the executive about both of them, I shared that Hank could use a bit more self-awareness and willingness to take feedback. That was met with a chuckle. "Just like his old man!" the executive said. "That's why I always liked his dad, and it's exactly why I'd probably like the kid too. We need that kind of restlessness here. I believe he probably could be an account manager within a year or so if he sets his mind to it!" When we discussed Betty, the executive said that he liked her but had some concerns she hadn't done sales and that it would probably take a while observing her work to gain a better sense of her accomplishments and what she could do in the future. What the executive keyed in on with Hank was his projection of confidence and restlessness. What he keyed in on with Betty was her humility and the highlighting of perceived gaps in skill. The executive assumed Hank's restlessness would lead to future success but assumed Betty's humility in her stated skills would lead to future failure. The organizational system, which was reflected by the executive's behaviors and mindset, likely reinforced Betty's already held subconscious feelings of imposter syndrome.

This example is not unique and is interesting on many levels, touching on unconscious bias, differences in gender styles, and blind spots leaders can have. However, for our purposes, let's unpack this situation further within the context of imposter syndrome. As we learned in earlier chapters, imposter syndrome can surface in many different ways. Because of Betty's concern with perfectly matching up with the position's requirements and a heightened focus on the required experience she felt she lacked, this no doubt impacted her presentation of herself. The self-sabotage of highlighting what she felt was lacking is a very common symptom of imposter syndrome.

The point isn't to determine whether Betty should have ignored the fact that she didn't meet every single qualification or if she should have overstated her abilities. Instead, culturally, it's up to leaders to be diligent about their own bias and blind spots. It's critical they make sure that they are not contributing to a culture where men are measured on their potential and women are measured on their performance, and to ensure they're not perpetuating a need for women to oversell themselves in order to get noticed. While many executives will say that they don't do this type of comparison, actions speak louder than words, so make sure that your actions count in the way you intend.

While women shouldn't hold themselves back and instead should take risks and be OK putting themselves out there even before they might be technically ready, organizations must ensure fairness in the assessment of people being considered for roles and base decisions on facts and not preferences. When they do so, the entire ecosystem works better.

Find Your Fierce Exercise: When delivering workshops on the topic of imposter syndrome, I tell a story about a job description that gets posted. A man and woman look at the same job to determine if they should apply. The woman looks at a bulleted list of ten qualifications. She analyzes her experiences and says, "Well, I've done eight of these things and I'm learning number nine in my current role. I haven't done number ten yet, though, so I better wait until I can show I'm qualified." A man looks at the list and says, "I've done six of these things, two of them I would delegate to someone else, and the other two? Well, I'm sure they don't expect a perfect candidate. I'll throw my hat in the ring!"

As an individual, reflect on how you have determined your readiness for a new role in the past. Are you more like the woman above or more like the man? Have you ever held yourself back from applying for a job because you didn't think you were qualified? Further, if you are a leader within an organization, what is your reaction to people who are downplaying their skills or seem to lack self-confidence? Do you take it at face value, or do you seek to better understand their experiences and qualifications more fully?

SUPPORT IS DIFFERENT FROM ACCESS

Support is important and takes on many forms. Companies must support a fair and equal opportunity for people to gain the experiences and sponsorship needed to rise to leadership positions. But while support is good, it can be passive. You can be supportive of someone developing, but it is a different story to open doors and create access for them. Access creates inclusivity and ultimately sponsorship.

Several years ago, I was in a position where I was coaching the senior-most people in a large, global organization. I was literally surrounded by some of the absolute best leaders I've ever had the privilege to work with, people who wanted to do right by their employees and spoke outwardly about the importance of diversity and inclusion. One day I was talking to Tim, a senior leader who happened to be, spoiler alert, a white male. I shared with him that I was working on a book about the topic of imposter syndrome, and he asked me to explain more. I shared a good deal of what I've shared with all of you so far in this book. After listening, he said, "Oh . . . yeah, I've had that." I asked him to tell me about a recent time he felt imposter syndrome.

Tim said that when he had been promoted to one of the top ten positions in the company—a title reserved for a very, very select few—he was *sure* they had made a mistake. While he knew his stuff and knew the industry inside and out, he was also *very* sure that the board of directors and senior-most leaders in the organization had made a mistake when they picked him. And, furthermore, it was only a matter of time before someone found out what a horrific fraud he was and banished him back to the ranks of middle management. Of course that didn't happen, but what he described definitely sounded like imposter syndrome. I asked him what he did when he felt these strong feelings of imposter syndrome start to sneak up on him. If I could learn what successful men did to fight the fraud and find their fierce, perhaps I could relay that to the female executives that I was coaching too. This is where it got interesting.

Tim said, "The first thing I did was call Bob. He's a good friend and someone I've worked with for the last twenty years. I thought he would be helpful because he had also recently been named to the top ten leaders." Bob's office was just two short doors away, so Tim walked over to his office and explained how he was feeling. Bob reflected to him what he knew to be true about Tim. "You are one of the smartest people I know," Bob said to Tim. "You demonstrate that every day. You turned around that business that was struggling in 2012, and you are extremely well respected by your employees. I've personally sought counsel from you many times myself in the last several years. I wouldn't be where I am today without you."

A few months went by, and the heat was turned up when the board of directors started questioning Tim about his bullish predictions on one of their businesses.

He felt like a fraud. Like he didn't belong. Like it was only a matter of time before someone figured out he wasn't as great as they thought he was and they would fire him . . . pronto. I asked what he did. He said, he knew Bob would just say more of the same things to him, and while he valued his input, he needed to call in the big guns. He knew the CEO very well. In fact, they'd also sort of grown up together in the corporate ranks. Tim gave him a call.

Just like that.

On speed dial.

He called the CEO.

And the CEO picked up the call.

Tim told him that he felt like maybe he (the CEO) had made a mistake and that Tim wasn't the best person for the role. Tim was having some self-doubt. "I've watched you grow and develop into a stellar leader," the CEO said. "Heck, we worked side by side on several business turnarounds between 2002 and 2010. That's almost a decade. I know your shortcomings and your strengths, and I'd place any bet that you are the *right* person for this role." Tim went back to his desk head held high, thinking, *Yep, I've got this.*

To give him a sense of how the story may have played out had Tim been more of an outsider, I asked him to replay the order of events, this time pretending that he didn't personally know the CEO, that he hadn't come up the ranks with him, and that the CEO did not know all of his strengths and shortcomings. Lastly, I asked him to pretend that he didn't have a friend in Bob to walk down C-Suite Row to bare his soul to when he was feeling insecure. What would have happened? What might be different? He looked at me like a deer in headlights. He stammered. He was apologetic. Then, he simply said, "Oh, I get it."

This is not a story about how Tim is wrong, or how Bob is wrong, or how the CEO is wrong. This is simply an illustration about the importance of access when navigating the corporate world. Tim is a very evolved and forward-thinking leader. Without much hesitation, I'd work for him again, especially now that his eyes have been opened and he is open to learning about his own definitions of success and how closed off they may have been to anyone who didn't look like him, sound like him, or follow a path like his. But until we had this conversation, he was operating from the standpoint of his experiences. Instead, this is a story about self-awareness, challenging ourselves to remove blind spots, leading the way, and creating access for all. Those behaviors level the playing field and enable people to quiet their inner critic and stop feeling like they don't belong.

This section focused on the access Tim had and how it shaped his trajectory and helped him move quickly through his feelings of imposter syndrome. But please don't underestimate the importance of general support too. Throughout the interviews for this book, many people shared that having a mentor and someone they could disclose their fears to was one of the most critical ingredients to their success. Having a support network and someone who had their back and was advocating for them when they weren't in the room was key. And having people who would tell it like it is, stand up and speak out, and verbally and visibly support leveling the playing field made all the difference. If you are a leader who wants to change your organization, please show your support *and* provide equal access to all the voices around the table. If they aren't at the table, bring them in.

> **Find Your Fierce Exercise**: As an individual, do you ask for access to leaders or simply seek their support? If you are a leader in an organization, evaluate the areas where you are outwardly supporting a program or initiative. That is a great first step. Now evaluate if you are taking every step you can to level the playing field, particularly with people different from yourself, and invite them in for true access.

LET PEOPLE KNOW DIFFERENCES ARE VALUED

For decades women have been told to mimic men to achieve success in the workplace. However, the solution to fighting imposter syndrome in organizations is not to be more homogeneous. It's important to verbally and visibly show that you value differences. Sounds easy enough, but when push comes to shove, when there is pressure from the board and you have to show results, sometimes the path of least resistance is the path taken.

Women tend to be natural systems thinkers, believing the whole is greater than the parts and engaging a broad group to solve problems. Men excel at immediate problem-solving and moving quickly, often in an individual manner. When systems work in individual ways, they may be short-sighted or less complete, but problem-solving might be faster and "good enough for now." Research has shown that women outperform their male counterparts in areas of teamwork, engagement, and leadership because they are focused on the whole and not only their individual parts. Yet what often is recognized within organizations is speed to solution and quick results. Organizations fall victim to the blind spot of short-term results. While they say long-term results are valued, what gets rewarded are the heroics and the diving catch.

The immediacy of a problem the business faces can take the focus away from what is actually needed, which is a holistic solution that could very well be more sustainable and far reaching. What can happen is that businesses will reward the "just-in-time" solution. This is a resolution that can, in many cases, cause more problems for the system at large in the long run.

Differences can feel like a temporary slowdown to progress. When you work with someone who is thinking and acting like you, things move quickly. It's effortless. But having different perspectives makes sure that the solution will stick longer and solve more broad-reaching problems. To accomplish this requires that we have a diversity of people around the table, diverse ideas, and diverse styles. How do we get that if people question their belonging when they are different? Businesses might say that they value differences and innovative, out-of-the-box thinking, but at the end of the day, the results that get measured are the short-term, quarterly, profit-oriented solutions. A diversity of approaches in terms of thinking and problem-solving would help to resolve this, and valuing the different ways a problem can be solved might negate the need for a diving catch.

An organization needs to value the differences inherent in their population, and one key way to do that is to communicate what you value outwardly and overtly. Think all-employee meetings where you are recognizing good work, or about whom you reward long-term stock options to. A spot bonus is a great way to reward and recognize a short-term solution, but when they want to signal a long-term behavior and outcome is valued, organizations must be overt about sharing that recognition with the rest of the company. Employees pay close attention to this. It's like a currency, and its value is increased each time a leader says what is good and valued. Employees are keeping score and taking note.

Find Your Fierce Exercise: Think about a time when you needed to quickly solve something and traded a systems approach for a quick win. What happened as a result? Were there any ramifications to that approach? Sometimes it doesn't feel like we have the luxury to include diverse perspectives. But as I always say, "No one has time to do it right, but everyone makes time to do it over." Was there anything about your scenario that required you to do rework after a while to get the best outcomes? Could you go back now and recognize the diversity of approaches to the problem and let people know that it was a learning that would be valuable to apply in the future? It's never too late to learn from past mistakes, even if in the moment they don't appear to be a mistake. Remember, growth mindset!

LISTEN DIFFERENTLY

How we use language is one observable difference between people that can fly under the radar and be a subtle trigger for imposter feelings. When describing accomplishments, efforts, or ideas, women often use the word *we*. Men, on the other hand, frequently use the word *I*. In what is a typically female collaborative approach, women blend ideas and build off each other, so the efforts produced are a result of the whole group coming together with input and wisdom. When women leaders share what the group came up with, they often use the word *we* to describe their accomplishments. Men will often acknowledge that the team worked together but will describe the results using *I* language, regardless of which ideas came from the group and which were their own individual contributions. Let's review a situation where this came to light.

I was in a group discussion with some colleagues, and the goal of the meeting was to come up with a recommendation for organizational structure to present to the leadership team. One of my colleagues, Susan, spoke up right away and addressed the group. "We only have about an hour, and it will be important for us to have a clear recommendation and path forward by the end of this meeting. Would everyone be OK if we started with one idea from each of us as a brainstorm and then we can narrow down from there?" Everyone agreed, and she grabbed the marker and captured all the ideas.

After about forty minutes, Karl said, "There are only twenty minutes left in the meeting, and I want us to really focus. I think it's super important that only the very best ideas are narrowed down and considered for inclusion in the recommendation." He grabbed the marker and went to the flip chart to circle a few ideas. "I propose the group consider this one, this one, and this one."

Both Susan and Karl helped the team move forward. Both offered ideas and opinions. The leadership tone Susan expressed when she used the word *we* was more communal. When Karl spoke, his tone was more individual. This isn't necessarily a problem by itself, but when you watch how the next part of the situation unfolded, it becomes more of an issue.

Fast-forward to the meeting with the leadership team a few days later. Susan and Karl were both in the meeting, and because they led the group discussion, they spoke on behalf of the team. The proposal went smoothly over- all. Both used the same speech patterns they used in the premeeting. Susan cited the group effort, the various ideas the team came up with, and how the group came to the conclusion they did. Karl also discussed the ideas and then wrapped with, "I don't see how there's any other solution that would give us the results this company needs. I highly recommend this solution, and I'm excited to hear your thoughts." Ultimately, the leadership team agreed with the final recommendation of the team and everyone walked away pretty happy.

After the meeting, I overheard a couple members of the leadership team talking in the hallway. They com- mented on Karl's passion and conviction for the solution. One even said, "You could hear how much this meant to him and how much he believed in it." Inadvertently, Susan was somewhat forgotten. The project team felt very included and happy with Susan's representation of their work. In fact, in a subsequent meeting, one colleague commented that she felt Karl took too much credit for the team effort. Yet Karl walked away standing out in the eyes of leadership.

The communal approach actually yielded a more in- clusive outcome for the project team, yet the *I* statements are what garnered the attention from the leaders. The point of the story is not that Susan should learn how to say *I* more, it's that leaders have an opportunity to listen differently. Celebrate collaboration and teamwork. Be OK knowing that a group effort doesn't mean that it's a weaker effort. It's actually often stronger.

CREATE A CONSISTENT EXPERIENCE

Men and women are having very different experiences in the workplace. These disparities in experience are further highlighted when you pay attention to the messages and advice that leaders share when reflecting on their own experiences. At one particular event I watched a panel of senior leaders share their insights and wisdom with a group of early-career rock stars—the best and brightest talent in the organization. There were two men and two women on the panel, and their advice to the audience was drastically different.

The men said things such as, "Just show up and do good work and the rest will fall into place. I never asked for a raise or a promotion, I let my work speak for itself. My sponsors knew me, and when the results were there, they knew they came from me." Conversely, the women advised, "Always be prepared. People are going to try to poke holes in your business case, but if you've done your homework, you can react and respond. You may not get another chance to shine, so make sure it counts."

The different mindsets at play were striking. The men

shared many examples of how they had sponsorship. This allowed them to operate from a place of abundance. They felt comfortable taking risks and focusing on doing good work. The women talked about how people tried to knock them down and how hard they had to work to be perfect. They appeared to be operating from a scarcity mindset.

One audience member stood up and asked what she could do to build her confidence. "I know my stuff, and I feel like a confident person overall, but I second-guess myself and hold back from speaking up," she said. She revealed that she worried when she was in a big meeting and the stakes were high that other people wouldn't see how smart she was. She worried that she would be exposed as a phony.

One of the male panelists responded with this advice: "Confidence really grows from doing your best work and having a willingness to learn from your mistakes and failures. Failure is the best professor." He had a growth mindset working for him, enabled by the organization.

What he said was certainly true; however, if people are operating from a place of scarcity, they don't want to speak up. They're afraid to fail. As the women on this panel showed, they feel they might not get another shot if they weren't perfect. There was a very different mental model at play here.

To quickly reflect on the "Listen Different" section: "*I* worked hard," when spoken by a male colleague, is taken as gospel, and he's applauded. He did great, these are obviously all his ideas, give that man a raise. "*We* worked hard," spoken by a female colleague, is met with confusion. Hmmm . . . who did what? Who should be rewarded? Did she even do any work? This ties in directly to the experiences that had been shared by male and female leaders in the panel discussion.

These experiences—in the same organization—were vastly different. Worlds apart. I have never met a woman in a leadership role who would advise a fellow woman to "just show up and do good work." But if you're reading this and in a leadership position currently, how could you reframe your approach to those working for you to ensure this experience isn't replicated?

INTENT VERSUS IMPACT

Microinequities feed imposter syndrome. Several years ago I used to travel the world visiting different business sites and office locations to meet with leaders regarding their people initiatives. One day, I had a meeting with a business leader named Jacob. He was well known in the business, had been the leader for quite some time, and was a bit "old school" in his thinking and actions, but most excused his quirkiness because of how successful he had made the business. Knowing that going into my meeting with him, I felt "ready" to work around those considerations.

That day I walked to his office, which was quite grandiose, and when I arrived, he was sitting at his desk. When he saw me, he waved and motioned toward a chair on the other side of his desk. I walked in and approached his desk, extending my hand for a handshake. He seemed surprised but obliged. It felt awkward. I thought to myself, *Isn't this what you do with business colleagues, especially those you don't know that well? Why was he so taken aback by my handshake? Did I give off an impression like I was too good?* My voices continued in my head until I finally just had to tell them to shut up.

After a few minutes of chitchat another colleague of ours, Bill, joined us for the meeting. Bill and Jacob worked together closely and were quite comfortable with each other. As we discussed the business at hand, whenever Jacob would respond to a question from me, he would talk toward Bill. I think it was out of habit, perhaps feeling more comfortable talking to him than to me. I found this to be a bit odd, and even though I knew that Jacob was quirky and sometimes socially awkward, the voice in my head kept telling me I was the outsider and I was the one who didn't belong. By about halfway through the meeting, I had myself believing that they didn't view me as deserving to be in the conversation and that something I was doing was wrong. They didn't greet me the same way they greeted each other, and they weren't responding to me directly. I wholeheartedly don't believe that was the intention, but that was the impact.

About forty minutes into our meeting, another person named Rick walked in. Jacob rose to his feet, extended his hand for a handshake, and said "Rick, great to see you." Rick, the business's finance person, worked closely with Jacob and saw him regularly. It was interesting to me that Jacob immediately shook his hand, almost as gentleman equals, but was surprised when I extended my hand for a similar handshake. Again, instead of feeling irritated by the microinequity that was demonstrated (although I am now after the fact), in that moment I took it on myself that I had done something wrong and didn't belong. The point is that I've been conditioned, however unconsciously, to chalk these situations up to something I'm doing or not doing. The conclusion I drew was that I didn't belong, and maybe they were figuring out that I was a fraud sitting at the table with them. It may sound silly to some, but all that was derived from a handshake and some eye contact during a conversation.

The handshake and eye contact example is one where the microinequities that occurred had a significant impact on me. Jacob's actions spoke volumes to me, and what I heard in his actions was that I was not equal. If you are reading this as a leader in an organization, reflect on your behaviors, particularly with the people you are most comfortable with. Do you create an environment where someone feels they don't belong? This story could have been included back in chapter 10 where the concept of microinequities was first introduced. However, identifying and combatting microinequities and unconscious bias is a deep-rooted issue for organizations. This is not a quick fix but one that is critically important to change in order to be inclusive and not have people feel they don't belong.

A wise woman once told me that we judge ourselves by our intent, but we are judged by the impact we have on others. It's time to tune in to the impact we are having. The signals sent are often so subtle that even the most evolved leaders don't see them or notice when they are sending them.

MENTORING IS GOOD; SPONSORSHIP IS BETTER

One *Harvard Business Review* study conducted in-depth interviews with men and women who were experiencing success climbing the corporate ladder to understand what kind of hurdles they faced as well as the types of help or support they received along the way. A different kind of support emerged that had a critical distinction. They found there was a significant difference between mentorship and sponsorship. The study found that "there is a special kind of relationship—called sponsorship—in which the mentor goes beyond giving feedback and advice and uses his or her influence with senior executives to advocate for the mentee." The study found that women are being "over-mentored and under-sponsored" in comparison to their male peer groups. That was one of the key factors identified in why women weren't advancing as quickly in their organizations. The study further pointed out that without this critical sponsorship, women are not only less likely to get those top jobs with big responsibilities, they are also less likely to even throw their hat in the ring for them. In short, if you want to help women advance and overcome any feelings of not belonging, consider putting your efforts toward sponsorship over basic mentorship.

I'm often asked what the key differences are between sponsorship and mentorship. I can see how they might seem similar. After all, both have "ships" in them. But that is about where the similarities end. Some differences: Mentorship is like speed dating. Sponsorship is like marriage. Mentorship is programmatic. Sponsorship is a mindset. Mentorship is a nice-to-have add-on to getting more women and minorities into the pipeline. Sponsorship is the need-to-have key to getting more women and minorities into the pipeline.

With mentorship, there is room to test the waters, impart wisdom, and decide if it's a fit. There is low investment in the grand scheme of things. You can try it out and see if there's a fit, and if there isn't you move on until you find someone you click with. There are fleeting moments of wisdom shared and valuable, in the moment, coaching that is received. Sponsorship is more like a marriage. There is skin in the game. People stick their neck out for the other person and there is a higher investment. At the end of the day, when you endorse someone and sponsor them, your brand is riding on it. This person is your ride or die. They won't be everyone's cup of tea, but you are willing to convince them otherwise. You believe in the person. Which is why it's relatively hard to have sponsorship 'programs'. As a sponsor, you don't focus on recency (unless you want that marriage to fail, pronto), you focus on the long haul—you believe in them. While it might sound like a BIG commitment to move from the world of speed dating to marriage, we do this all the time in the professional setting, but we do it with those people we are most comfortable with—our peeps. Which is what takes the pressure off the act of sponsoring someone. When we are doing it, we rarely call it "sponsorship"; instead it's those times when we facilitate an introduction to a senior leader. We bring their name up in a meeting to get them some airtime. We endorse the quality and effectiveness of their work. This is sponsorship. Even if we get a slight side-eye, we persist. We believe in the person. The funny thing is that we actually do this all the time. We don't label it as such, we just do it. And the issue is that as humans, we have unconscious bias, so we tend to sponsor those who look like us, sound like us, and have followed similar paths as we have. It's our comfort zone. It's our preference. This is why it's so critically important to have what I call responsible sponsorship, where the sponsor is consciously aware of who they are sponsoring and for what purpose. If we do this, we have a shot at more diverse sponsorship relationships that open doors and provide access to diverse sets of people. To have preference and bias doesn't make us bad people, it makes us human. But as leaders, if we don't keep that preference and bias in check, it can cause big problems. We continue to advocate for and sponsor the same people over and over again. This creates less diversity in the pipeline. This act of standing up for and behind those you sponsor opens doors and provides access in a way that we don't often think about when we are doing it. It's powerful.

Think back to chapter 6, where senior men were beginning to cite a reluctance to mentor women since the #MeToo movement. If mentoring is of concern to men, sponsorship may be even harder to encourage. This further illustrates why it is so important for the business environment and culture to adapt to the realities of the modern workplace. This includes treating everyone with respect, being comfortable around people who are different from you, and ensuring a level playing field. It is not OK for men to simply say they are uncomfortable meeting with women one-on-one because of the optics. If there is concern, meet with the office door open or in a public place. Whatever is decided, make sure it's applied consistently for men and women.

Throughout the book, I have not pointed fingers or called out any one group as a source problem feeding imposter syndrome feelings for those people in the minority. That said, this is one area I am going to ask the leaders in the majority (aka white men) to rise to the challenge, because you have the power to fix this. Because white men still hold the majority of top jobs in corporate America, you are in the best position to advocate differently and actively sponsor all talent, particularly those people who are most different from you. By doing so, you will change the culture. You will level the playing field and drive equal opportunities for advancement. You will allow for a sense of belonging that women and minorities have not always felt, and not having that sense of belonging fuels imposter syndrome.

CONCLUSION

Regardless of who you are, whether you've experienced imposter syndrome acutely or through someone else, I hope the stories and articulations of the systems that feed imposter syndrome for others moved you. It will take all of us to change the systems we are a part of to make progress, to help those who are suffering, and to be inclusive and make sure everyone feels like they belong. This is not a singular challenge with a singular cause. It's complex. So too is the path forward. If you don't want to suffer from imposter syndrome, the first thing to start with is yourself.

I'm often asked the question, Why do *I* have to change? It feels unfair that *I* must change and speak differently, or show up differently, because of the way I'm judged or perceived. If we know the problem exists within our systems, why don't *they* change? Agreed. It's unfair. A wise person once asked me if I wanted to be right or if I wanted to be happy. Over time, our systems will change and evolve to be truly more equal for people to bring their whole selves and not feel like they are being evaluated every day. That said, at the rate we are going currently in order to get stronger female representation at the top of the house in Fortune 500 organizations, we won't experience gender parity for another ninety-five years. That is the math if the calculations and projections are correct. Sadly, that won't be in most of our lifetimes.

This doesn't mean we shouldn't fight to change things and try to accelerate the pace of that change. However, it does mean that we need to find ways to be happy and stop beating ourselves up to fully own the success that should be ours, today. When trying to change things, it's important to meet the person or organization where they are. Be aware of the listening you are speaking into, and bring them along on the journey. It's like coaxing a scared pup out of the woods . . . one tasty nugget at a time. If we want organizations that are open to changing and being truly inclusive, we need to change our thinking and our actions to change the outcomes we are getting.

It's both fascinating and frustrating to recognize that you can be in a space of expertise about imposter syndrome and still fall victim to it. It's like you are running a low-grade fever all the time. You know what you need to do to feel better, and at times you are even doing them. Yet in those moments of quiet self-candor, you wonder when the shoe is going to drop and you're going to be found out as a fraud. I have lived this experience intimately.

Not long ago, I was asked to step into a bigger role at the company I was working for. I would be leading a strategy that would have the eyeballs of the senior-most leaders on it. The pressure was dialed way up. Not only was the team size increasing, but the level of professionals I'd be leading was also higher. I would be leading other executives who likely weren't going to need my daily coaching and would be working pretty autonomously. Intellectually, I felt a little nervous about the challenge but ultimately up to the task. As I settled in, my new normal became long hours and high-pressure presentations. I got super busy and found that I was leaving less and less time in the day for Interruption and Momentum strategies. The voice of the imposter got a lot louder.

I noticed the voice growing louder for me while preparing documents for the board of directors. I'd be second-guessing my facts and wondering if they would question my authority to be speaking on the topic. When I would go to preparation sessions for these large meetings, I would agonize over the details, sometimes missing the big picture. When a senior leader would ask a question in the meeting that I thought I should have already addressed, I would beat myself up over it for hours after the meeting. I was not in a good place.

After some time, I realized that I needed to practice what I was preaching and check in with the frAIMwork. I was certainly aware of what imposter syndrome was and how it showed up. Now, I needed to pay attention to what was happening and follow the steps to interrupt the negative voices and get back to the momentum groundwork I had already laid regarding my values and value. I started to ask myself, *What if that's not true?* when

I was beating myself up over not knowing an answer and feeling like I should have. I started to bring forward my ideas that I was perhaps too fearful to bring up previously, even though I knew they were good ideas. And, most important, I shifted my thinking to realize that even though something was obvious to me it was a unique value only I could bring. It made me feel powerful and like I belonged. And you know what? It worked. Awareness is not enough—you have to interrupt the fraud in the moment and take steps toward your long-term fierce momentum.

Think of the practices in the Interrupt and Momentum sections of this book as medicine that can help you fight off that low-grade fever of imposter syndrome. When you spike a fever, you take aspirin to bring it down. But your vitamin C will help you not get sick in the first place. When you do these practices, they will create a mindset that can serve you in the moments you really need it—when you get that hard feedback or make a mistake. Instead of blowing up a mistake in your mind and making it ten times larger than it is, when you do the practices advised, it makes it easier to put things into perspective so you can be more resilient and resourceful.

A lot has changed in the ten years since I started writing this book, including some amazing female writers exposing the bullshit that we have operated under for many years. When I read their stuff, I feel enlightened and empowered. The messages to accept yourself are inspiring and important. Yet when I walk back through the doors of corporate America, if I'm being 100 percent honest, I don't always feel as fierce. Why is that? The books tell us to take up space, be bold, and feel brave. But the systems close in around us, and it is hard to be strong and fierce on a daily basis. I want to feel different, and I believe there is a lot more room to actually be fiercer. I am optimistic that we can get there, but we aren't there yet. I believe that is because it isn't just about each individual needing to shift their thinking and actions, it's about the systems that we are all a part of and the immense influence they have on us every day.

If you are one of the brave people willing to acknowledge that parts of this book struck a chord for you, even if you aren't entirely sure why, that's awesome. The goal with this book was not to expose anyone or make them feel bad for how they are feeling. That said, many fantastic people are simply not in tune with their feelings. They feel frustrated, conflicted, or stuck but have not examined why. For anyone willing to be curious about imposter syndrome and how it might be showing up in your lives, a huge round of applause is coming your way. Hopefully over time, people won't experience imposter syndrome at all. Until then, we will continue to fight the good fight and make sure you don't get stuck with a limiting set of beliefs that set you on a course for limited actions and limited results. Instead, you are now on a course to *being fierce*!

ACKNOWLEDGMENTS

As you know, it's taken over ten years to write this book. It was hard work, and I am in awe of those people who write for a living. Back when the idea for this book was just a twinkle in my eye, I sensed there was a need for it but had no idea where to begin. So many people have helped me along the way, and I would be remiss if I didn't give a shout-out to them now as the twinkle has grown from a little light to a full-blown fire in the belly and passion for helping people find their fierce. I'm going to do the thing where I call out some people by name, but I know I'm going to forget someone, and truth be told, so many people have invested in me and cheered me along as I went. I can only say, you know who you are, and truly, truly, thank you.

The journey has taken twists and turns that I would not have anticipated, but I wouldn't change anything about it. At times, I beat myself up for how long it was taking and the many times I set it on the shelf—sometimes for a year at a time. In fact, had I written it ten years ago, it would be a very different book. So much is different in the world versus ten years ago, and since then many,

many courageous women have brought a voice to issues that should no longer be swept under the rug or deemed acceptable. I'm grateful to the likes of Amy Cuddy, Brené Brown, Jessica Bennett, Sheryl Sandberg, Tara Mohr, Jen Sincero, Amy Poehler, and so many other authors who have been bold, unapologetic, *fierce* female role models for me—God, I love you ladies, and I dream of meeting you one day. (Actually, I had the privilege of meeting Amy Cuddy at an event once, so I'd say I'm off to a good start, LOL.) Honestly, had the book been published ten years ago, it would have been more theoretical and had a lot less wisdom in its pages. That wisdom comes not only from my own personal experiences climbing the ladder and fighting the fraud feelings, but also from the extraordinarily wise people in my crew who have shared their light with me—some directly, many indirectly, but I've taken it all in, let it soak, and poured it into this resource to help as many others as I can. A particular shout-out to Jacque, Dara, Becky, Marci, Tara, Heidi, Angela, Tim, Shveta, Colleen, Kelly, Derek, and Emily—your stories and insights throughout brought to life the concepts and the learnings. Thank you for sharing your time and support so generously and freely. And to the many mentors and sponsors I've had along the way, I wouldn't be where I am without you.

Countless friends and family members have cheered me on, learned with me, taught me, and provided much-needed encouragement throughout this process. Thank you for understanding when I missed things because I was writing or editing or researching or interviewing. And, perhaps most important, thanks for listening to me talk about "the book" for a decade. I seriously owe you and appreciate your support more than you know.

And my biggest thanks to my husband, Erik. You believed in me far more than I believed in myself and have never once made me feel like anything less than a rock star. Through the starts and stops of this project, you reminded me every day that it didn't matter where I was or how quickly I got to the finish line; it was about putting one foot in front of the other, even on the days I didn't want to. When I needed help with anything from figuring out the best way to publish, to reading chapters out loud, to wiping my tears during the occasional stress meltdown, to celebrating every single damn milestone along the way no matter how big or small—you were there. We are a true team. I don't know how I became so lucky, but I can only hope you know how special you are to me. This book is one heartfelt token of thanks. With all my heart, I dedicate it to you. Love you MORE!

REFERENCES

Abrams, Abigail. "Yes, Impostor Syndrome Is Real: Here's How to Deal With It." *Time*, Time, 20 June 2018, time.com/5312483/how-to-deal-with-impostor-syndrome/.

"Awareness." *Merriam-Webster*, Merriam-Webster, www.merriam-webster.com/dictionary/awareness?utm_campaign=sd.

Bak, Per. *How Nature Works*. Oxford University Press, 1996.

Barlow, Rich. "BU Research: A Riddle Reveals Depth of Gender Bias: BU Today." *Boston University*, 16 Jan. 2014, www.bu.edu/articles/2014/bu-research-riddle-reveals-the-depth-of-gender-bias/.

Bennett, Jessica. *Feminist Fight Club*. Portfolio Penguin, 2017.

Bohannon, Audra, et al. "Women in Leadership." Edited by J. Evelyn Orr, *Talent Management Best Practices Series: Women in Leadership*, The Korn/Ferry Institute, 2013, www.kornferry.com/content/dam/kornferry/docs/article-migration/Best-Practices-Women-in-Leadership.pdf.

Cannon, Walter B. *The Wisdom of the Body*. Norton, 1967.

Caro, Tim, et al. "Benefits of Zebra Stripes: Behaviour of Tabanid Flies around Zebras and Horses." *PLOS ONE*, Public Library of Science, 20 Feb. 2019, journals.plos.org/plosone/article?id=10.1371%2Fjournal.pone.0210831.

Church, Zach. "The Quiet Discrimination of Microinequities: A Q&A with Adjunct Professor Mary Rowe." *MIT Sloan*, 3 Feb. 2016, mitsloan.mit.edu/ideas-made-to-matter/quiet-discrimination-microinequities-a-qa-adjunct-professor-mary-rowe.

Clance, Pauline Rose, and Suzanne Ament Imes. "The Imposter Phenomenon in High Achieving Women: Dynamics and Therapeutic Intervention." *Psychotherapy: Theory, Research & Practice*, vol. 15, no. 3, 1978, pp. 241–247., doi:10.1037/h0086006.

Concordia University. "Surprising Truth about Obsessive-Compulsive Thinking." *ScienceDaily*, ScienceDaily, 8 Apr. 2014, www.sciencedaily.com/releases/2014/04/140408122137.htm.

Coury, Sarah, et al. *Women in the Workplace 2020*, McKinsey & Company, 30 Sept. 2020, www.mckinsey.com/featured-insights/diversity-and-inclusion/women-in-the-workplace.

Cuddy, Amy Joy Casselberry. *Presence: Bringing Your Boldest Self to Your Biggest Challenges*. Little, Brown Spark, 2018.

Davis, Hank. "The Uptalk Epidemic." *Psychology Today*, Sussex Publishers, 6 Oct. 2010, www.psychologytoday.com/us/blog/caveman-logic/201010/the-uptalk-epidemic.

"Digest of Education Statistics, 2018." *National Center for Education Statistics (NCES) Home Page, a Part of the U.S. Department of Education*, U.S. Department of Education, Sept. 2018, nces.ed.gov/programs/digest/d18/tables/dt18_318.30.asp?current=yes.

Doidge, Norman. *The Brain That Changes Itself: Stories of Personal Triumph from the Frontiers of Brain Science*. ReadHowYouWant, 2017.

Dweck, Carol. *Mindset the New Psychology of Success*. Random House, 2016.

Eilperin, Juliet. "White House Women Want to Be in the Room Where It Happens." *The Washington Post*, WP Company, 13 Sept. 2016, www.washingtonpost.com/news/powerpost/wp/2016/09/13/white-house-women-are-now-in-the-room-where-it-happens/.

"Employment Status of the Civilian Noninstitutional Population by Age, Sex, and Race." *U.S. Bureau of Labor Statistics*, U.S. Bureau of Labor Statistics, 22 Jan. 2020, www.bls.gov/cps/cpsaat03.htm.

Foroudi, Layli. "How Organisations Are Tackling Gender Bias." *Financial Times*, Financial Times, 20 Sept. 2018, www.ft.com/content/87586758-99a0-11e8-88de-49c908b1f264.

Fry, Richard. "U.S. Women near Milestone in the College-Educated Labor Force." *Fact Tank: News in the Numbers*, Pew Research Center, 20 June 2019, www.pewresearch.org/fact-tank/2019/06/20/u-s-women-near-milestone-in-the-college-educated-labor-force/?utm_source=AdaptiveMailer&utm_medium=email&utm_campaign=19-06-20%2Bwomen%2Bin%2Blabor%2Bforce%2BFT&org=982&lvl=100&ite=4253&lea=982361&ctr=0&par=1&trk=.

Gevinson, Tavi. "I Want It to Be Worth It: An Interview With Emma Watson - Page 2 of 5." *Rookie*, 27 May 2013, www.rookiemag.com/2013/05/emma-watson-interview/2/.

Gorlick, Adam. "Media Multitaskers Pay Mental Price, Stanford Study Shows." *Stanford News*, 24 Aug. 2009, news.stanford.edu/2009/08/24/multitask-research-study-082409/.

Goudreau, Jenna. "Women's Achilles' Heel: The Vision Thing." *Forbes*, Forbes Magazine, 11 July 2012, www.forbes.com/2009/04/01/workplace-boss-career-women-leadership-vision.html#179082166a5c.

Greenspon, Thomas S. *Moving Past Perfect: How Perfectionism May Be Holding Back Your Kids (and You!) and What You Can Do about It*. Free Spirit Pub., 2012.

Hanson, Rick. *Hardwiring Happiness: the New Brain Science of Contentment, Calm, and Confidence*. Harmony Books, 2016.

Harris, Russ. *The Confidence Gap: from Fear to Freedom*. Robinson, 2011.

Heitler, Susan. "How Gender Differences Make Decision-Making Difficulties." *Psychology Today*, Sussex Publishers, 2 Feb. 2012, www.psychologytoday.com/us/blog/resolution-not-conflict/201202/how-gender-differences-make-decision-making-difficulties.

Horton, Anisa Purbasari. "The Five Types Of Impostor Syndrome And How To Beat Them." *Fast Company*, Fast Company, 29 Nov. 2018, www.fastcompany.com/40421352/the-five-types-of-impostor-syndrome-and-how-to-beat-them.

Huang, Jess, et al. "Women in the Workplace 2019." *McKinsey & Company: Featured Insights*, McKinsey & Company, Oct. 2019, www.mckinsey.com/featured-insights/gender-equality/women-in-the-workplace-2019.

Huber, Jennifer. "How Does Media Multitasking Affect the Mind?" *Wu Tsai Neurosciences Institute*, 19 Oct. 2018, neuroscience.stanford.edu/news/how-does-media-multitasking-affect-mind.

Hunt, Vivian, et al. "Delivering through Diversity." *Organization: Our Insights*, McKinsey & Company, Jan. 2018, www.mckinsey.com/business-functions/organization/our-insights/delivering-through-diversity.

Ibarra, Herminia, et al. "Why Men Still Get More Promotions Than Women." *Harvard Business Review*, 7 Sept. 2017, hbr.org/2010/09/why-men-still-get-more-promotions-than-women.

Ibarra, Herminia. "A Lack of Sponsorship Is Keeping Women from Advancing into Leadership." *Harvard Business Review*, 11 Oct. 2019, hbr.org/2019/08/a-lack-of-sponsorship-is-keeping-women-from-advancing-into-leadership.

James, Willaim. *The Principles of Psychology*. Holt, 1915.

Krivkovich, Alexis, et al. "Women in the Workplace 2018." *McKinsey & Company: Featured Insights*, McKinsey & Company, Oct. 2018, www.mckinsey.com/featured-insights/gender-equality/women-in-the-workplace-2018.

Later, W, et al. "Is the 1975 Reference Man Still a Suitable Reference?" *European Journal of Clinical Nutrition*, vol. 64, no. 10, 2010, pp. 1035–1042., doi:10.1038/ejcn.2010.125.

Lee, Linda-Eling, et al. "Women on Boards." *Women on Boards: Global Trends in Gender Diversity on Corporate Boards*, MSCI ESG Research Inc., Nov. 2015, www.msci.com/documents/10199/04b6f646-d638-4878-9c61-4eb91748a82b.

Liswood, Laura. "How Men and Women See Gender Equality Differently." *World Economic Forum*, 15 Nov. 2015, www.weforum.org/agenda/2015/02/how-men-and-women-see-gender-equality-differently/.

Markway, Barbara G., and Celia Ampel. *The Self-Confidence Workbook: a Guide to Overcoming Self-Doubt and Improving Self-Esteem*. Althea Press, 2018.

Matthews, Gail, and Pauline Rose Clance. "Treatment of the Impostor Phenomenon in Psychotherapy Clients." *Taylor & Francis*, Psychotherapy in Private Practice, 5 Nov. 2010, www.tandfonline.com/doi/abs/10.1300/J294v03n01_09.

Mattson, Mark P. "Superior Pattern Processing Is the Essence of the Evolved Human Brain." *Frontiers in Neuroscience*, vol. 8, 22 Aug. 2014, doi:10.3389/fnins.2014.00265.

Mejia, Zameena. "How to Combat 'Hepeating' at Work, According to a Harvard Professor." *CNBC*, CNBC, 11 Oct. 2017, www.cnbc.com/2017/10/11/how-to-combat-hepeating-at-work-according-to-a-harvard-professor.html.

Mezzofiore, Gianluca. "Women Are Less Likely than Men to Receive CPR in Public. A New Product Is Designed to Change That." *CNN*, Cable News Network, 5 June 2019, www.cnn.com/2019/06/05/health/female-cpr-dummy-women-cardiac-arrest/index.html.

Mineo, Liz. "Less Stress, Clearer Thoughts with Mindfulness Meditation." *Harvard Gazette*, Harvard Gazette, 17 Apr. 2018, news.harvard.edu/gazette/story/2018/04/less-stress-clearer-thoughts-with-mindfulness-meditation/.

Mohr, Tara. *Playing Big: Practical Wisdom for Women Who Want to Speak up, Create, and Lead.* Avery, an Imprint of Penguin Random House, 2015.

Nayyar, Sarita. "How to Support More Women in Leadership Roles." *Global Agenda: Gender Parity*, World Economic Forum, 8 Mar. 2020, www.weforum.org/agenda/2020/03/international-womens-day-women-leadership-roles/.

Neff, Kristin. *Self-Compassion: Stop Beating Yourself up and Leave Insecurity Behind.* William Morrow, 2015.

Neff, Kristin. *Self-Compassion: the Proven Power of Being Kind to Yourself.* William Morrow, an Imprint OfHarperCollinsPublishers, 2015.

Noland, Marcus, et al. "Is Gender Diversity Profitable? Evidence from a Global Survey." *PIIE: Working Papers*, Peterson Institute for International Economics, 31 May 2019, www.piie.com/publications/working-papers/gender-diversity-profitable-evidence-global-survey.

"Not Harassing Women Is Not Enough." *Key Findings*, Lean In, 2019, leanin.org/sexual-harassment-backlash-survey-results.

Oppland, Mike. "8 Ways To Create Flow According to Mihaly Csikszentmihalyi [+TED Talk]." *PositivePsychology.com*, 12 Oct. 2020, positivepsychology.com/mihaly-csikszentmihalyi-father-of-flow/.

Podrazik, Joan. "WATCH: The Surprising Ways You Express Fear Without Realizing It." *HuffPost*, HuffPost, 8 Apr. 2013, www.huffpost.com/entry/what-is-fear-dr-brene-brown-and-oprah_n_2876633.

Poehler, Amy. *Yes, Please!* Pan, 2018.

Premack, Rachel. "17 Seriously Disturbing Facts about Your Job." *Business Insider*, Business Insider, 2 Aug. 2018, www.businessinsider.com/disturbing-facts-about-your-job-2011-2.

"Quick Take: Women in the Workforce - United States." *Catalyst: Research*, Catalyst.org, 5 June 2019, www.catalyst.org/research/women-in-the-workforce-united-states/.

Ritter, Meredith, and Kathryn Graff Low. "Effects of Dance/Movement Therapy: A Meta-Analysis." *The Arts in Psychotherapy*, vol. 23, no. 3, 1996, pp. 249–260., doi:10.1016/0197-4556(96)00027-5.

Samuel, Sigal. "A New Study Finds a Potential Risk with Self-Driving Cars: Failure to Detect Dark-Skinned Pedestrians." *Vox*, Vox, 5 Mar. 2019, www.vox.com/future-perfect/2019/3/5/18251924/self-driving-car-racial-bias-study-autonomous-vehicle-dark-skin.

Sandberg, Sheryl, and Marc Pritchard. "The Number of Men Who Are Uncomfortable Mentoring Women Is Growing." *Workforce and Employment: Gender Parity*, World Economic Forum, 20 May 2019, www.weforum.org/agenda/2019/05/the-number-of-men-who-are-uncomfortable-mentoring-women-is-growing/.

Schumann, Karina, and Michael Ross. "Why Women Apologize More Than Men: Gender Differences in Thresholds for Perceiving Offensive Behavior." *Psychological Science*, vol. 21, no. 11, 2010, pp. 1649–1655. *JSTOR*, www.jstor.org/stable/41062429. Accessed 2 Dec. 2020.

Segal, Gillian Zoe. "This Self-Made Billionaire Failed the LSAT Twice, Then Sold Fax Machines for 7 Years before Hitting Big-Here's How She Got There." *CNBC: Power Players*, CNBC, 3 Apr. 2019, www.cnbc.com/2019/04/03/self-made-billionaire-spanx-founder-sara-blakely-sold-fax-machines-before-making-it-big.html.

Silva, Christine, et al. "Report: Good Intentions, Imperfect Execution? Women Get Fewer of the 'Hot Jobs' Needed to Advance." *Catalyst: Research*, Catayst, 2012, www.catalyst.org/research/good-intentions-imperfect-execution-women-get-fewer-of-the-hot-jobs-needed-to-advance/.

Simon, Phil. "The Empress Has No Clothes: An Interview with Joyce Roche." *HuffPost*, HuffPost, 7 Dec. 2017, www.huffpost.com/entry/the-empress-has-no-clothe_b_3601497.

SNYDER, W. S., et al. *Report of the Task Group on Reference Man: a Report Prepared by a Task Group of Committee 2 of the International Commission on Radiological Protection: Adopted by the Commission in October, 1974*. Elsevier Science, 1994.

Stolberg, Sheryl Gay. "Female Senators, Their Ranks Increasing, Reflect on Breaking Into the Boys' Club." *The New York Times*, The New York Times, 16 Apr. 2018, www.nytimes.com/2018/04/16/us/politics/collins-ernst-klobuchar-heitkamp.html.

Warner, Judith, and Danielle Corley. "The Women's Leadership Gap." *Center for American Progress: Women*, Center for American Progress, 21 May 2017, www.americanprogress.org/issues/women/reports/2017/05/21/432758/womens-leadership-gap/.

Warner, Judith, et al. "The Women's Leadership Gap." *Center for American Progress: Women*, Center for American Progress, 20 Nov. 2018, www.americanprogress.org/issues/women/reports/2018/11/20/461273/womens-leadership-gap-2/.

Wheatley, Margaret J. *Who Do We Choose to Be?: Facing Reality, Claiming Leadership, Restoring Sanity*. Berrett-Koehler Publishers Inc., 2017.

Winfrey, Oprah. "What Oprah Knows About the Power of Meditation." *Oprah.com*, Aug. 2016, www.oprah.com/inspiration/what-oprah-knows-about-the-power-of-meditation.

Young, Valerie. "Frauds on the Red Carpet? True Confessions of Academy Award Winners." *HuffPost*, HuffPost, 28 Apr. 2013, www.huffpost.com/entry/impostor-syndrome_b_2760878.

Young, Valerie. *The Secret Thoughts of Successful Women Why Capable People Suffer from the Impostor Syndrome and How to Thrive in Spite of It*. Three Rivers Pr, 2012.